THE NAZIS AND THE OCCULT

THE DARK FORCES UNLEASHED BY THE THIRD REICH

PAUL ROLAND

ACKNOWLEDGEMENTS

The author wishes to acknowledge the following as primary sources of background information and quotations:

Dr Felix Jay, article in *Traditional Astrologer* magazine (1998); Francis King, *Satan and Swastika* (Granada Publications, 1976); Peter Levenda, *Unholy Alliance* (Continuum, 2002); Nigel Pennick, *Hitler's Secret Sciences* (Neville Spearman, 1981); Hermann Rauschning, *Hitler Speaks* (Howard Fertig, 1939); Hermann Rauschning, *Voice of Destruction* (Kessinger, 2004); Trevor Ravenscroft, *The Spear of Destiny* (Sphere, 1990); Lewis Spence, 'Occult Causes of the Present War' (Kessinger, 1998); Gerald Suster, *Hitler and the Age of Horus* (Sphere, 1981); Wilhelm Wulff, *Zodiac and Swastika* (Barker, 1973).

This edition published in 2018 by Arcturus Publishing Limited
26/27 Bickels Yard, 151–153 Bermondsey Street,
London SE1 3HA

AD006181UK

Printed in the UK

THE NAZIS
AND
THE OCCULT

Contents

Introduction

When my father surveyed the destruction of Nazi Germany in 1946 as part of the Allied Army of Occupation, he shared the belief held by the victors that they had defeated a formidable military machine and liberated a population who had been living under a totalitarian dictatorship since Adolf Hitler's accession to power in 1933. During the war, Churchill, Roosevelt and even Stalin – who it later transpired had murdered even more of his own people than had Hitler – joined with religious leaders in describing the Second World War in apocalyptic terms as being a battle between the forces of light and darkness, a struggle between Good and Evil for the soul of the civilized world. But this was considered merely religious and political rhetoric.

At that time, conventional historians attributed the rise of Nazism exclusively to socio-economic factors and that remained the accepted view for the next twenty years. Hitler had appeared at a time of national crisis to haul a demoralized Germany off its knees following the inglorious defeat of the First World War and restore its national pride. He brought it through a decade of political instability and ruinous inflation by ruthlessly eliminating the opposition and borrowing far beyond his country's means. Hitler has been called a shrewd political strategist, but in truth he simply did as he wished and damned the consequences. In crude terms he was spoiling for a fight. His inner demons demanded constant stress, adoration and attention like a spoilt child. Once in power he refused to pay the punitive reparations imposed on Germany by the victors and he rebuilt his armed forces in defiance of the Versailles Treaty which was intended to limit German rearmament. Then he marched into the occupied Rhineland, annexed Austria and snatched back the Sudetenland, half hoping for a reaction from an outraged international community – again the action of a petulant bully. But this only earned him the admiration of his people and the grudging respect of other world leaders who would like to have been equally self-assertive.

It was not only the fascist leaderships in Spain and Italy who openly admired Germany's ability to get its own house in order, but many European aristocrats who shared Hitler's suspicion of the Jews whom they regarded as having far too much control of the financial infrastructure. And despite their initial dislike of the petty bourgeois Austrian corporal, German industrialists also came to embrace the New Order, grateful for the revitalization of the German economy – particularly the armaments industry on which many had built their fortunes and family names.

By the time Germany hosted the Olympic Games in Berlin in 1936, the nation was regarded as a model of reconstruction and regeneration, and was looked upon with envy by Britain and America – as well as by its long-time enemy France – all of whom expressed their regard for the German qualities of resourcefulness, industry and organization. As for the Nazis' persecution and disenfranchising of the Jews, made legal by the iniquitous Nuremberg Laws, this was excused as being the

This picture bears all the hallmarks of the Nazis' propaganda department as adoring supporters look to Adolf Hitler, fresh from being elected Chancellor of Germany in 1933, for leadership.

excessive zeal of a regime which would come into line with its neighbours in due course.

The worst their critics would say was that the Nazis were political opportunists and street brawlers whose strutting leaders affected cultural pretensions which they never possessed, inviting comparison with America's gangsters. But no one seriously believed that there was anything more sinister at work behind the scenes than rabid nationalism – not until the full extent of Nazi atrocities were revealed to the world at the Nuremberg trials. Disbelief at the scale of the wholesale murder of millions and the clinical efficiency with which it had been perpetrated led even the most dispassionate observers to describe the Nazis as evil and Hitler's power over his people as messianic.

But no one seemed able to answer the questions which the revelations of Nuremberg had raised: namely, how could a cultured nation which had produced Goethe, Beethoven, Bach, Schiller, Einstein, Kant, Hegel and so many of the world's greatest thinkers and artists allow itself to be led lemming-like to the precipice of self-destruction by a ragged collective of criminals, misfits, sadists and petty bureaucrats – the very dregs of its society? And why did that society so readily fall for the blatant propaganda perpetrated by men who shamelessly appealed to their basest instincts? Moreover, how could one explain the enigma of the demagogue himself? As the respected British historian A.J.P. Taylor remarked: 'How could a man so ignorant, so enslaved by stupid dogmas, have achieved such practical success?' It seemed inconceivable that a man of Hitler's limited imagination, intellect and avowed indolence could have galvanized a nation into following him blindly where he willed, unless there was something else empowering him which the people sensed and entrusted with their fate. In short, what was the true nature of the regime that had raised Germany from defeat to be master of Europe and thence to wholesale destruction in less than 12 years?

It was not until the occult revival of the late 1960s that interest in the Third Reich and its possible link with black magic gave birth to a slew of sensationalist 'alternative' histories and fictional accounts of Nazi associations with 'dark forces'. Popular culture of the period reflected the public's morbid fascination with the more sensational aspects of the supernatural, spawning such films as *Rosemary's Baby*, *The Exorcist*, *The Omen* and *The Boys from Brazil*, in which mad Nazi doctor Josef Mengele successfully cloned young boys from cells taken from Hitler's body.

But the horrors were not all confined to fiction. The Age of Aquarius dawned to reveal the sadism inflicted by Nazi-loving Charles Manson and his devil-worshipping groupies, together with the ravages wrought on an entire generation by drug addiction and the horrors televised daily from Vietnam. Overnight the hippies' psychedelic dream darkened and disillusionment set in. Many began to question the nature of evil and wonder if the devil and his disciples really did exist. And if evil was a conscious entity actively seeking entry into our world, could that account for the nightmare of Nazism from which the world was just beginning to awaken?

In the past fifty years, a number of writers have claimed to have uncovered the truth concerning Hitler's pact with some diabolical agency, but in the main they have merely exploited our persistent morbid fascination with the Third Reich and perpetuated the myth of Nazi involvement with the occult. It is the purpose of this book to demystify these dark fairy tales and reveal the true nature of Nazi Germany's link with arcane influences and of evil itself.

I have drawn extensively on secret Nazi documents and the private diaries and correspondence of Hitler's 'satanic' mentors, as well as those of the members of his inner circle to reveal whether Nazi ideology was indeed rooted in occultism.

The intention of this book is to explain how an ill-educated, psychologically unbalanced nonentity succeeded in mesmerizing an entire nation, why the German people venerated their Führer as a god and how he exercised his power over them to the extent that they were willing to follow him to the abyss of self-destruction.

Forget what you have read, seen and heard. This is the real secret history of the Third Reich and its dark Messiah – Adolf Hitler.

Chapter One

THE DARK GURUS

'The motivating power, then, in all magical operations, is the trained will of the magician. All the adjuncts of Ceremonial Magic – lights, colours, circles, triangles, perfumes – are merely aids to concentrating the will of the magician into a blazing stream of pure energy.'

Francis King, *Ritual Magic in England*

Ritual magic is the act of communicating with the subconscious to empower the practitioners with the attributes required or to influence providence to provide them with what is desired. By definition then, black magic is the art of influencing another person to do your bidding by imposing your greater willpower on their subconscious and, ultimately, to create the world in your image. By this definition, Hitler and the leading Nazis were intuitive black magicians. But the art of magic in itself is neither good nor evil. It is the intention behind the desire that determines whether one is working with the universal laws or manipulating them for one's own ends. The circles, symbols and stagecraft have no inherent power of their own – it is the impression these rituals produce on the psyche which effects results. But magic is not a 'quick fix' that promises something for nothing. As with any other demanding spiritual discipline every magical operation is subject to the law of karma (the law of cause and effect), which states that whatever you put in will come back to you.

Magic is natural to mankind, not supernatural. In its most subtle form it is evident in the art of seduction when one attempts to impress a prospective partner through eye contact, subtle facial expressions, body language and an alluring intonation in the voice; physical attraction on its own is rarely sufficient. The same ritual can be witnessed in its most primal and potent form in the animal kingdom when certain predators literally 'fascinate' their prey by their hypnotic movements until they are ready to strike.

Magic is not a relic of the Dark Ages. It has been, and continues to be, practised every day by ordinary men and women in civilized societies, as well as in so-called 'primitive communities'. However, unless the individual is an adept who has consciously performed a ritual to create a specific effect, the results are invariably attributed to luck, fate, personal charisma or coincidence.

Magic, in its truest sense, is at the core of every creative act, every desire that we bring into physical manifestation, from conceiving children to planning our home. It is also part of the process by which we draw upon our latent strengths whenever we 'psych ourselves up' to perform extraordinary feats or 'pluck up the courage' to face something we fear. However, for most of us, wishes and daydreams dissolve into the ether when we return to reality because we have not learnt how to focus our mental energy and sustain the image we wish to bring into being. In contrast, magicians empower their desires with sufficient vital energy by focusing their mental and emotional resources on this specific object. This then takes on a reality in the higher worlds and eventually manifests in our material world in the form envisaged.

Ritual magicians employ various theatrical effects to assist them to get 'into character' to perform what is effectively the central role in a modern 'mystery play' – a sacred act in which they identify with a god who personifies a specific attribute that they wish to awaken within themselves. If they wish to strengthen their intuitive powers, for example, they will assemble artefacts corresponding to the Moon, the planetary body associated with that aspect of their personality. They will decorate their room with curtains of the colour corresponding to the chosen planet and place associated objects on the altar, again to attune them to that quality which that planet represents. Even the incense will be chosen to focus the magician's mind on this single principle. The conjurations will then be carried out in a consecrated circle sealed with sacred signs and symbols which define the magician's sphere of influence. In such an atmosphere, the magician's consciousness will be raised from the mundane to a higher state of awareness – a greater reality where the real inner work of transformation can be done.

Ambitious and successful individuals invariably achieve what they aspire to because they practise this form of 'inner temple' magic, now known to Jungian psychologists and New Age gurus as 'creative visualization'. Hitler possessed a vision of himself as leader of Germany and he ensured that he was in the right place at the right time to seize the opportunity that he had created. His sense of destiny and of being protected by providence was nothing more than his intuitive sense of his own ability to manipulate people and events that were within his sphere of influence. The most obvious demonstration of this ability was the staging of the Führer's public appearances at the Nuremberg Rallies. When he withdrew from public life during the war, his power diminished and his acolytes were reduced to squabbling among themselves. But the Nazis have not been the only organization to exploit the power of ritual mass manipulation.

With their effective use of music, lights and sexual imagery, rock concerts can be as potent as any pagan rite. Religious organizations also acknowledge the value of ritualized worship – the use of candles, incense and symbols, and the hypnotic quality of prayer to create a sense of unity climaxed with the sharing of some form of sacrament – which is as theatrical and potentially transforming as any magical ceremony. Even political parties and commercial corporations practise a crude form of magic when they use a memorable symbol or slogan to implant or enforce the desire for whatever it is that they are selling, be it commercial merchandise or an ideology. Nevertheless, in modern times few movements have used ritual magic and its attendant paraphernalia as effectively as the Nazis.

What made them even more dangerous was the fact that they were unaware that they were doing so and, consequently, were unable to control the forces that they had invoked. Such forces have been traditionally envisaged as demons and devils, but they are merely the manifestation of our unconscious fears and desires.

It is not necessary to believe in the existence of evil as a conscious entity to unleash it. The intention to dominate and manipulate is sufficient, for evil is entirely man-made. The Nazi hierarchy were intuitive magicians who exercised their will over the German nation by their unconscious exploitation of powerful arcane symbols, evocative music, quasi-religious ritual and, most significant of all, cultural archetypes.

ARCHETYPES

Archetypes are universal figures which personify abstract qualities, characteristics or ideals such as the Hero, the Villain, the Mother, the Father, the Magician, the Witch (or the Seductress). They are common to all cultures around the world and feature in myths and folk tales where they represent specific personality types that are likely to be encountered in real life. They occasionally appear in our dreams because they can embody a specific aspect of our own personality or that of other people we have encountered, and because they are a universally recognized symbol they have a strong resonance in our subconscious. By invoking certain archetypes the Nazis appealed directly to the nation's deepest fears and aspirations.

For example, they didn't need to appeal to the intellect to rationalize their persecution of the Jews. All they needed was to depict the Jew as a hideous figure intent on deflowering Aryan maidenhood to trigger the desired response in Aryan men.

Similarly, the Nazi propagandists only had to invoke the image of Siegfried who was the personification of Teutonic manhood, to awaken the latent hunger for comradeship, adventure and combat in every young German male whenever they needed more volunteers for the SS or the *Wehrmacht*.

Hitler was not an attractive man, but he evidently held a particular fascination for women which was not solely due to the power he wielded, nor to his personal magnetism which would only affect those in his immediate presence.

For those in his thrall he personified the father figure, a

symbol of authority and protection, while for others of a more mystical mindset he fulfilled their hope for a messiah, a saviour. To Germany's enemies he was the personification of evil, the archetypal trickster – or the Antichrist for those of a biblical bent. Clearly, he could not have been all of these.

More likely, he was none of them. He was a blank canvas on to which both his admirers and his enemies could project the archetype of their own choosing and that is what made him such a potent symbol.

Carl Jung, the father of modern psychoanalysis, believed that Hitler had the ability to address the Teutonic archetypes who symbolized the primal forces in the German psyche – Wotan (*aka* Odin), Thor and the Lords of Chaos. Jung suggested that these gods were revitalized by contact with Hitler and erupted from the Collective Unconscious to lead the nation to war.

THE DAWN OF THE MAGICIANS

'Natural magic or physical magic is nothing other than the deepest knowledge of the secrets of nature.'
Del Rio, 16th century

The true meanings of the words 'magic' and 'occult' are misunderstood by those outside the esoteric tradition. In the popular imagination they evoke lurid images of men in voluminous robes adorned with exotic symbols conjuring demons from the abyss, or cackling old hags cavorting naked under the full moon. Such scenarios are, however, the invention of the medieval mind and specifically of the early Church which created the devil and his disciples to frighten followers of the 'old religion' into abandoning their beliefs and instead put their faith in a messianic saviour who promised to redeem them from original sin.

Despite the recent rekindling of interest in paganism and the paranormal, such superstitions and a general wariness of the occult still persist today. It is no wonder then that few can accept the idea that Hitler and his Nazi regime might have been practitioners of the black arts. They cannot imagine the brown-shirted bullies of the SA (*Sturmabteilung*) and the black-uniformed legions of the SS (*Schutzstaffel*) forming a satanic coven, or Hitler and Himmler standing in a magic circle uttering the 'barbarous words of invocation' to guarantee world domination. But if the original meaning of the word 'occult' is understood to mean simply 'that which is hidden or unknown' and a truer definition of magic is 'that which involves the exercising of the will to bring about a change that would not occur naturally', then a compelling case can be made for Hitler having practised black magic and the Nazi era being the manifestation of demonic power.

Such a scene does not, of course, just appear like Mephistopheles at the adept's invitation. The stage must be set, the time of the ritual chosen to coincide with favourable alignments of the stars and the necromancer needs to prepare himself or risk being overwhelmed by the demonic forces he seeks to invoke. Such preparations were in place in Germany at the turn of the 20th century.

WARRIOR BREED?

As an idealistic young man Guido von List (1848–1919) believed himself to be the last in a long, illustrious line of Nordic warrior magicians known as the Armanen [after the chieftain Arminius], whose blond, blue-eyed ancestors had driven the Roman legions out of Germany. At the age of 14, he had knelt before a ruined altar in the crypt of St Stephen's Cathedral in Vienna, renounced his Catholic faith and committed himself to building a temple to Wotan. By the time of his death, he had honoured the promise of his youth in words though not in stone, by erecting an altar of ideas at which the nationalists could worship the gods of past glories – both real and imagined.

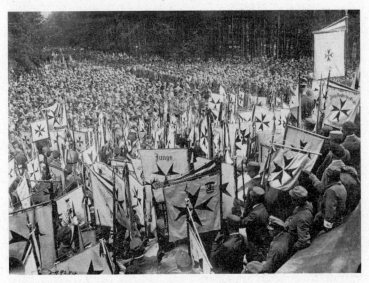

Banners of the Germanen Order, an early German nationalist, pseudo-mystical society founded along quasi-Masonic lines in Berlin in 1912, one of a rash of similar groups at the time.

Guido Karl Anton List was a tradesman's son who awarded himself the aristocratic appelation 'von', a habit shared by many of his occult brethren with upper-class pretensions. It is customary to portray him as a visionary, the mystically minded, bearded patriarch of the Ariosophist movement, a group of Vienna-based *völkisch* nationalists who sought to unify a divided nation by stressing its cultural identity at a time of political disunity. ('*Völkisch*' means 'of the people' and refers to a movement combining folklore, occultism and ethnic nationalism later espoused by the Nazis.) But such ideas betrayed the yearnings of dreamers, not scholars. In truth, the Ariosophists were a clique of hierophantic elitists whose dreams of an idealized past exemplified by chivalry and the nobility of rural life were tainted by virulent racism. A strong case could be made to support the allegation that the Nazis' anti-Christian sentiment originated with von List who accused the early Church of having first humiliated then persecuted the *Armanenschaft*, driving them out of Germany and demonizing their deities as satanic.

Moreover, the Ariosophists' entire ideological edifice was built on unstable ground. Von List's Armanenism, for example, was a wholly fictitious occult system – a wish-fulfilment fantasy founded on a misinterpretation of the central maxim of the Kabbalah (the Jewish mystical tradition) which states 'as above, so below'. Von List interpreted the maxim to mean that God created a hierarchy of superior and inferior beings which gave him a theological basis for justifying the conceit of Aryan (i.e., Teutonic) superiority, whereas the tenet is understood by true initiates to denote that the divine attributes are manifest in finite form in all mankind – regardless of race, creed or colour.

Von List also undermined his *Weltanschauung* (world view) by declaring that the mythical Armanen brotherhood had left philological clues to the location of their sacred sites in the place names of hills, rivers and towns, despite a lack of evidence to support this contention. He simply 'read into' place names whatever he wanted to find and ignored sites which did not conform to his theory. Moreover, many of his assertions were made on the basis of his visions, not fact. While walking up the Hermannskogel, north of Vienna, and again while camped out at the Geiselberg hillfort, he claimed to have had a vision of his ancestors performing rites and it was these clairvoyant glimpses into the past on which he based his thesis. Had he poured his considerable energy and imagination into writing fiction, he might have enjoyed a reputation equal to that of the Gothic novelist Edward Bulwer-Lytton, who fed the fantasies of the proto-Nazis in novels such as *The Coming Race*. Instead he was born in the age of the irrational when anyone who claimed to have 'channelled' the arcane wisdom of the ancients or read the secrets of life and death in the Akashic Records (an invisible matrix of mental energy) would find a receptive audience.

The first years of the 20th century had seen an explosion of interest in psychic phenomena and Eastern philosophy as a reaction to the prevailing materialism and modernity. This interest found expression in the fashionable new 'religions' of Spiritualism and Theosophy. Madame Blavatsky, co-founder of the Theosophical movement, had proudly boasted that she had taken dictation, while in a mediumistic trance, from her 'hidden masters' who existed on a higher spiritual plane. The result was the voluminous *Secret Doctrine* (1888) which introduced the concept of a superior prehistoric Atlantean race to the world. So when von List published the first of his Aryan ideological tracts, *German Mythological Landscapes* (1891), such ideas were not only in vogue, but its author could rest assured that he would not be pressed to provide evidence for his pronouncements. In such circles, psychic insight was seen to be as valid as empirical research, if not more so, and insights received in trance were considered as unassailable as the visions of the prophets. His admirers clearly thought of him in those terms and gathered together to form the Guido von List Society in 1908 with the aim of promoting his works around the world.

At the second annual conference of the Theosophical Society, held in London in 1905, a German admirer, von Ulrich, introduced von List's theories to a receptive worldwide audience. 'Love of the Fatherland,' said von Ulrich, 'was among the virtues of the German peoples and he who loves his Fatherland loves his past, which is, indeed, only the mother of the present.' Von List's success was assured.

However, it seems von List's prophetic powers cannot be as readily dismissed as his visions of the past. Towards the end of the Great War, he predicted that those who had given their lives for the Fatherland would be reborn to lead a nationalist revolution and wreak revenge on the Allies. They would be led by a *Starke von Oben* (Strong One From Above). The year would be 1932. On that point, at least, von List was not far from the truth.

THE GERMANEN ORDER

Von List's mystical neo-paganism was evidently not pragmatic enough for his disciple, Philipp Stauff, who was one of the principal members of the Germanen Order which was founded in 1912 and whose stated aims were the 'monitoring of the Jews and their activities' and the distribution of anti-Semitic material – specifically the group's own rabidly racist magazine *Hammer* which, they boasted, was their 'sharpest weapon against Jewry and other enemies of the people'.

Curiously, this anti-Semitic order modelled itself on the Freemasons, a philanthropic fraternity, who were accused of being an agency of the mythical 'worldwide Jewish conspiracy'. Despite being prey to internal squabbling as various egos fought for control of the group, the order played a significant role in creating the climate which nurtured the Nazi Party. Even so, the crank element was also in evidence in the form of a racial physical examination which was performed in Berlin by phrenologist Robert Berger-Villingen and his patent 'plastometer' machine. Applicants were required to submit to an exhaustive series of cranial measurements to determine their racial purity, after which the successful candidates were permitted to take part in an initiation ceremony which mixed elements of the Hermetic

Order of the Golden Dawn (an occult group founded in 1888), Freemasonry and scenes from Richard Wagner's operas.

The novices were led blindfold into a candlelit ceremonial chamber where the Master of the Lodge, flanked by two members dressed in knight's robes, awaited them. The Knights wore horned helmets and leant on their swords barring the entrance to the uninitiated. In front of them the Lodge Treasurer and Secretary sat at a table wearing white masonic sashes while in the centre of the room stood a Herald. At the rear of the room, in the area which represented the Grove of the Grail, stood the Bard and the Master of Ceremonies, the former robed in white, the latter in blue. Around the latter stood the brothers, forming a semicircle as far as the Treasurer's table. At the far end of the room in an antechamber a choir of 'forest elves' sang to the accompaniment of a wheezing harmonium. As the novices waited without, the brothers broke into the 'Pilgrim's Chorus' from *Tannhauser* then greeted the Master of Ceremonies by making the sign of the swastika which he solemnly returned. This signalled the ushering in of the novices who heard a speech by the Master of Ceremonies introducing the aims of the order and laying out its Ario-Germanic ideology. The Bard then lit the sacred flame and the novices took off their blindfolds and robes to stand naked before their brethren. The ceremony climaxed with the Master presenting the spear of Wotan to the prospective candidates who answered his invocations while music from *Lohengrin* rose, accompanied by the elfin choir.

It is no wonder that Hitler later condemned such theatrics

as the impotent posturing of pseudo-mystics in a speech to the 1938 Reich Party Congress.

'At the pinnacle of our programme stands not mysterious premonition, but clear knowledge and hence open avowal. But woe if the movement or the state, through the insinuation of obscure mystical elements, should give unclear orders. And it is enough if this lack of clarity is contained merely in words. There is already a danger if orders are given for the setting up of so-called cult-places, because this alone will give birth to the necessity subsequently to devise so-called cult games and cult rituals. Our cult is exclusively cultivation of that which is natural and hence willed by God.'

From the Germanen Order emerged yet another phoney aristocrat, Baron Rudolf von Sebottendorf (real name Adam Alfred Rudolf Glauer), who was to have an insidious influence on Nazi ideology. Sebottendorf, who drowned himself in the Bosporus in 1945 because he couldn't bear to see Germany in ruins, was unapologetic about his racist views which he made plain in his choice of name for his own faction, the Premier Anti-Semitic Lodge. Candidates had to prove that the purity of their blood went back three generations and submit to having their skull measurements taken to confirm their racial suitability. Such ideas were not, as one might expect, on the fringe of German politics but at its core. It is a popular misconception that the

Nazis instigated German anti-Semitism. The growth of this *völkisch* occult subculture demonstrates the existence of deep-rooted racism in Germany preceding the Nazi era. Hitler merely exploited it.

By the outbreak of the Great War there were some 100 Germanen Order lodges across Germany. When their younger members volunteered or were conscripted in 1914, they brought their racist ideology with them into the trenches. In the man-made hell of no man's land, these demonic evangelists found fertile soil in which to sow the bitter seeds of fascism.

ORIGIN OF THE SWASTIKA

One of the first periodicals to promote what could be called occult nationalism was funded by Sebottendorf. *Runen* (Runes) featured articles on occult science, earth mysteries, rune lore and racial somatology (a branch of anthropology concerned with physical characteristics). This was just one of a wave of occult literature published around the time of the Great War to satisfy a growing public appetite for esoteric knowledge and 'alternative' philosophies. These included *Der Wanderer*, *Prana*, *Theosophie* and *Neue Lotusbluten* as well as a glut of astrological periodicals and an influential series of books under the Osiris imprint. To promote his beliefs and his magazine, Sebottendorf sponsored a separate study group to explore the basis for belief in the lost continent of Thule, the Nordic

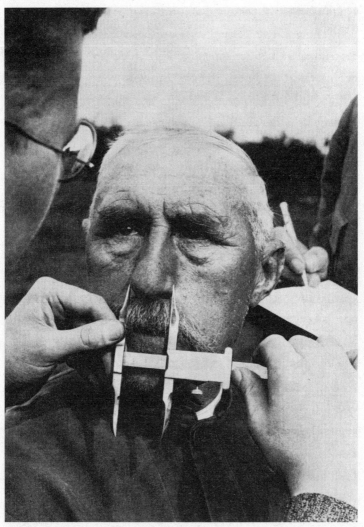

The racial purity tests that candidates had to pass in order to join the Germanen Order were updated by the Nazis to prove 'Aryan superiority'. Here, an ethnic German has his nostrils measured, 1941.

Atlantis, which he asserted was the origin of the Teutonic race. The Thule Society included future Nazi 'philosopher' Alfred Rosenberg and Hitler's mentor Dietrich Eckart; this prompted Sebottendorf to boast: 'Thule members were the people to whom Hitler first turned and who first allied themselves with Hitler,' although there is no evidence that Hitler attended any of their meetings.

The significance of the Thule Society almost entirely in their adoption of three symbols which were later to appear on Nazi regalia – a sword, an oak leaf cluster and the hooked cross more commonly known as the 'swastika'.

The origins of the swastika are unknown. All that can be said for certain is that it was used many thousands of years ago as a symbol of good fortune – its Sanskrit name *svasti* translates as 'all is well' – in countries as far apart as Peru, China, India, Tibet and Scandinavia. It is thought that von List may have been the first to appropriate it as a symbol of German nationalism having seen it featured in the stained glass windows of a Viennese church. He suggested that the swastika was a sacred Aryan symbol derived from the *Feuerquirl* (fire whisk) with which the universe had been created. But whatever its origin, it would have been familiar to occultists throughout Europe as the symbol of the Theosophical Society and to historians as a heraldic detail. During the Nazi era, a genealogical society gleefully unearthed the forgotten fact that the Prussian royal family had featured a swastika on its coat of arms. In 1891, Edward Hulme, author of *Symbolism in Christian Art,* had pointed out:

'In the use of the fylfot (the swastika's heraldic name) the early Christians merely adopted and diverted to their own purpose a symbol centuries older than the Christian era, a symbol of early Aryan origin, found abundantly in Indian and Chinese art ... it stands for the lightning wielded by the omnipotent deity, whether the deity be the Manu, Buddha or Brahma of the East, or the Thor or Zeus of the West.'

Its association with evil was known long before the Nazi era, but even the Theosophists could not decide which way round denoted malevolence and which the contrary. In a 1909 issue of the *Theosophical Review*, H. S. Green attempted to clarify the issue:

'Most readers will be aware that some difference of opinion exists as to the direction in which the cross is supposed to be turning ... whichever may be considered to be the correct way of drawing the symbol, the opposite one will stand for that which is contrary to the divine order, and so for evil in general and black magic in particular.'

Green noted that if the arms of the swastika were depicted as if turning anti-clockwise then it would denote the divine order which was the direction shown on the official seal of the Theosophical Society. Even so, this was the direction chosen by the Nazis. The opposite direction was said to symbolize the descending hammer of Thor, the Norse god of Thunder and therefore the destructive force. Clearly, the Nazis were either unaware of the significance denoted by its direction or they thought of themselves as crusaders against the evil, degenerate, subhuman, non-Aryan races and deliberately chose to depict the *Hakenkreuz* (hooked cross) turning in an anti-clockwise direction. Most likely, they simply didn't care. It was an instantly recognizable symbol – simple, stark and strong.

The swastika is thought to have first caught Hitler's eye as a boy when he attended school at Lambach, Austria in 1897. Each day he had to pass through the archway of the Benedictine monastery which bore the order's coat of arms featuring a swastika.

Twenty-three years later, when he was searching for a symbol for the party flag, he seized on the swastika which was central to a design drawn by dentist Friedrich Krohn, a member of the Germanen Order and its offshoot, the Thule Society. It featured a black swastika on a white circle within a red field – the white symbolizing national unity and the red representing the blood shed for the cause (although the official line was that the red represented the party's socialist aspirations). Krohn's swastika spun clockwise which Hitler insisted be reversed. Curiously, it is in the Jewish esoteric teachings known as Kabbalah, which forms the foundation of the Western magical tradition, that the counter-clockwise direction of the swastika as used by Hitler is understood to denote evil. Perhaps Madame Blavatsky thought that the subject did not merit further consideration – or perhaps she had higher matters on her mind.

INSIDIOUS INFLUENCES

'It would hardly be going too far to say that the horrors of Belsen and the ovens of Auschwitz were ultimately derived from the occult racial ravings of von Liebenfels and the tiny group of his followers who existed, like maggots in an apple, within the tolerant and civilized environment of Franz Josef's empire.'

Francis King, *Satan and Swastika* (1976)

Von List's most fervent disciple, Lanz von Liebenfels, was another counterfeit aristocrat. His real name was Adolf Josef Lanz (b. 1874), the son of a Viennese schoolmaster who yearned from an early age to establish a new 'Ario-Christian' religion over which he would preside as the supreme, unquestionable authority. He was obsessed with the pomp and pageantry of religious rituals and burned with a fanatical piety which was matched by an equally obsessive interest in sex. In 1893, at the age of 19, he had taken holy orders at the Cistercian monastery at Heiligenkreuz, but was defrocked for unspecified transgressions six years later. In a fit of pique he formed his own religious order, the Order of the New Templars, which was built on the belief that Good and Evil were at war in the world, the former being

Adolf Hitler with the 'Old Fighters', veterans of the unsuccessful 1923 Munich Putsch (coup), during the annual commemoration of the event. The rune on the banners signifies those who fell that day.

embodied in the Aryan, and the latter in their racial inferiors, the 'apelings'. The Aryans, said Liebenfels, worshipped the god Fraja Christus (a Gothic name for Jesus) who demanded the sacrificial slaughter of the sub-humans to purify the world. Once again, the parallels with the Nazis are striking.

It was Liebenfels who coined the term Ariosophy in 1915 – to encompass the philosophical outlook shared by the various *völkisch* occult groups who were active at the time – and who cited the main purpose of the movement as being the study of the differences between the 'blond' and the 'dark' races, the former being the embodiment of the 'pan-psychic' energy which animated all life on Earth.

In Liebenfels' scheme the Aryans were God incarnate, whose esoteric teachings and mastery of the occult sciences had been long lost through their descendants' preoccupation with technology and the pleasurable diversions of this world, specifically carnal knowledge of 'inferior races'. In so doing they had forfeited their rightful place in the natural hierarchy.

If Aryan man was to have a chance of reclaiming his birthright, Liebenfels declared, he must look for clues to justify his claim to power in the heraldic devices and names of his ancestors and also in the psychic record of history impressed on the ether (the Akashic Records), which could be accessed through such esoteric arts as palmistry and astrology.

Like von List, 'von' Liebenfels was possessed of a restless energy and intellectual curiosity, but unfortunately it was directed towards an unproductive and perverse end. Accordingly, he attempted to find a scientific basis for his religious beliefs by forcing the facts to fit his theory, discarding any evidence which proved inconvenient with a shrug, as if to say 'scientists will never fully understand the incomprehensible mysteries of God and his universe'. Hitler and his irrational 'philosophers' – Hörbiger, Wiligut and Wirth, to name but three – were to use the same argument to justify their wild fantasies which also flew in the face of the facts.

But while they waxed ecstatic over the possibility of unearthing archaeological evidence to support their belief in a race of prehistoric Nordic supermen, Liebenfels was getting hot under the collar at the thought of rampant sexual ceremonial rites in the forests of the Fatherland. He interpreted the story of the fall of man in the Bible as a warning against bestiality which he surmised had been the chief occupation of the chosen people (the Aryans) and the reason for their downfall.

Under this delusion he 'decoded' the Passion as the attempted rape of Christ by the pet pygmies of a satanic cult of beast-men who were devoted to interbreeding! This specious mix of theology and anthropology synthesized in a new and dangerous quasi-science that became known as 'theo-zoology'.

As the prophet of this new order it naturally fell to Liebenfels to write its bible.

He called it *Theo-Zoology or the Lore of the Sodom Apelings and the Electron of the Gods* (1905), a monomaniacal rant betraying the author's repressed sexuality and a hatred for women which almost rivalled that of his hatred for the Jews.

A central accusation in the persecution of the original Templars was their worship of Baphomet, above, a practice the Templars had supposedly acquired from 'Saracens' in the Middle East.

BESTIAL LUST

He damned women as weak for submitting so willingly to bestial lust (presumably only when it involved sex with a 'racial inferior') and urged that they should be conscripted as brood mothers in eugenic convents (*Zuchtkloster*) where they would be serviced by Aryan males to ensure the purity of the race.

In an effort to restrict the breeding of the inferior races, the state could order them to be forcibly sterilized, enslaved or even incinerated.

It's no wonder, therefore, that the Abbot of Heiligenkreuz refused his final wish to be buried within the monastery grounds.

When Liebenfels raised a swastika flag over the battlements of Werfenstein castle in 1907 to inaugurate his new order of Templar knights, his admirers believed they were witnessing the dawn of a new epoch in German history which would usher in a cultural and spiritual renaissance. Had they known what he would later write to a member of their order in 1932 they might not have been so eager to see that era come into being.

> *'Hitler is one of our pupils. You will one day experience that he, and through him we, will one day be victorious and develop a movement that will make the world tremble.'*

In fact, there is no evidence that Hitler was ever a member of the order, though it is possible that he and Liebenfels exchanged a few words one day in 1909 when Hitler reputedly called at the offices of *Ostara*, a magazine edited by Liebenfels, to purchase a number of back issues. But the source of this story was Lanz 'von' Liebenfels himself.

MAN AND SUPERMAN: WAGNER AND NIETZSCHE

'Whoever wants to understand National Socialist Germany must first know Wagner.'

Adolf Hitler

No history of the Third Reich, occult or otherwise, would be complete without at least a brief mention of two men who were a profound influence on Hitler and Nazi ideology – composer

Like Liebenfels, the 'irrational philosopher' Hans Hörbiger (1860–1931) was not interested in facts.

Richard Wagner and philosopher Friedrich Nietzsche. The former inspired Hitler with the idea that his war against the communists and Jews was a mystical crusade, while the latter provided him with the belief that there was an intellectual argument to justify his global ambitions and a logical basis for his fanatical beliefs.

> *'The German soul has passages and galleries in*
> *it, there are caves, hiding-places, and dungeons*
> *therein; its disorder has much of the charm of the*
> *mysterious; the German is well acquainted with the*
> *by-paths to chaos.'*
> Friedrich Nietzsche, *Beyond Good and Evil* (1886)

On the day Hitler was born, Nietzsche (1844–1900) had made a prophetic comment in his notebook: 'I know my destiny. Some day my name will be associated with the memory of something monstrous.'

He sensed that the complex philosophy outlined in *Man and Superman*, *Beyond Good and Evil* and *The Anti-Christ* would be distorted and corrupted by those who would seize on the superficial implications of what he had put forward rather than on the substance of his argument. In the last-named, he described Christianity as 'the most fatal, seductive lie that has yet existed' for promoting the idea that compassion and morality are superior to physical strength. By contrast, he argued, nature favours the ruthless and the powerful. 'The beast of prey and the jungle prove that evil can be very healthy and develop the body magnificently.' Only 'the warrior' is truly free. He equated democracy with mediocrity, degradation and the diminution of those whose strength of purpose should allow them to rule over the weak and live beyond the constraints of human concepts such as Good and Evil. Carried away by his vision of rampant self-determination, he described, 'the magnificent blond beast [of German manhood] roaming wantonly in search of prey and victory.' It was a phrase he lived to regret. Another was his call for an end to democracy and the establishing of a 'New Order' under a 'Master of the Masses'. 'One who will dominate and rule Europe – a frightening individual Will ... [that] will bring an end to the long spunout comedy of little states ... as well as democratic many-willedness. The time for politics is passed: the next century will bring the battle for the domination of the Earth ...'

But for all his urging of youth to throw off the shackles of conformity, he feared unlimited state control and anti-Semitism made him physically sick. 'It is a matter of honour with me to be absolutely clean and unequivocal in relation to anti-Semitism, namely opposed to it, as I am in my writings ...' He was also fiercely against German nationalism: 'Behold the Germans, the lowest, most stupid, most common race that exists on earth ...' Such sentiments were overlooked by the volunteers and conscripts who pored over *Also Sprach Zarathustra* in the mud of Flanders from 1914 to 1918. One line in particular no doubt escaped their notice. In prophesying the appearance of the 'Master of the Masses', Nietzsche had referred to him as 'the last man', because he would be the one to initiate Armageddon and this 'last man' he described as 'the most despicable'.

TWILIGHT OF THE GODS

'When I hear Wagner it seems to me that I hear rhythms of a bygone world. I imagine to myself that one day science will discover in the waves set in motion by the Rheingold *secret mutual relations connected with the order of the world.'*

Adolf Hitler, *Mein Kampf*

Wagner provided the musical setting for Hitler's vision of German global domination. His epic melodramas are a granite monument in music to the grandeur of Aryan superiority and sacrifice. Without Wagner's *Sturm und Drang* (storm and stress) tempered with pastoral interludes, Nazism would not have acquired its mythic undertones.

Both Theodor Reuss, a practitioner of Tantric sex magick, and Sar Peladan, the French writer on the occult, believe that Wagner was an intuitive magician. By drawing on Teutonic mythology and its Aryan archetypes, Wagner was able to attribute heroic qualities to German manhood and motherhood while demonizing their enemies. *Parsifal*, for example, which celebrated Christian mysticism in the tale of a knight's search for the Holy Grail, was conceived as a sacred

A scene from Richard Wagner's opera, Parsifal *(1882): Wagner's works became compulsory listening in the Third Reich because they were based on Germanic myths which encapsulated 'true German virtues'.*

'mystery play', a musical rite to be experienced rather than simply enjoyed as high art. Wagner stressed its secondary, or occult, function by insisting that performances be restricted to the opera house at Bayreuth, which later became a place of pilgrimage for Wagner connoisseurs who wished to share the sacrament with the composer.

Hitler acknowledged the magical element in the music when he remarked, 'For me Wagner is something Godly and his music is my religion. I go to his concerts as others go to church.' When listening to *Parsifal*, Hitler admitted to being 'transported' into an 'extraordinary state, a mystical dream world' in which he could endure the tensions of his turbulent nature.

In contrast to Nietzsche, Richard Wagner (1813–83) was an instinctive anti-Semite with no intellectual basis for his beliefs – his anti-Semitism erupted from professional jealousy. He despised his contemporaries Mendelssohn and Meyerbeer because he thought their music was frivolous, but he wasn't shrewd or sensible enough to criticize them for this. Instead, he attacked them on the basis of their religion as if the shallowness of their music was indicative of their race.

Wagner believed that he could establish a national cultural identity by creating great German art which would be an expression of the national spirit and its ideals. He thought he could only do this if he purged German art of its 'impurities' – by which he meant the Jewish element. In an effort to achieve this he adopted right-wing rhetoric and his countrymen's ingrained suspicion of 'the outsider' by pointing an accusing finger at the Jews whom he denounced as the embodiment of the abstract forces of modernity and social disintegration which exemplified everything he considered alien to the German soul.

His interminable rambling essays on race, politics and art had as deep and lasting an influence on Hitler as did his music, prompting one commentator to liken his pernicious essay

'Judaism in Music' (1850) to the lighted match an arsonist will toss into a room soaked with petrol. Wagner made it socially acceptable for educated Germans to be anti-Semitic and that alone damns him in the minds of many who cannot hear his music without recalling its more sinister associations.

Chapter Two

THE SPEAR OF DESTINY

'Though he who has boldly risen from the abyss through an iron will and cunning may conquer half the world, Yet to the abyss he must return. Already a terrible fear has seized him; in vain he will resist! And all who still stand with him must perish in his fall.'

Goethe, *The Awakening of Epimenides*,
Act II, Scene 4

On an overcast afternoon in early autumn 1913, a grim-faced, wretched-looking youth stood shivering outside the Hofburg Museum in Vienna's historical Heldenplatz with his sketch book and watched as the first spots of rain blurred his latest watercolour. At the time, Adolf Hitler was 19, practically destitute and in a state of almost constant despair. He had failed to gain admission to Vienna's prestigious Academy of Fine Arts or to the city's School of Architecture and was reduced to sharing a shabby single room with a childhood friend in a squalid part of the city. His dead mother's savings were almost spent and he had little prospect of earning a living from selling his postcard-sized pictures. Vienna's bourgeoisie shunned peddlers and, besides, Hitler's sketches were crude and characterless. He was suddenly forced to face the fact that his hopes of becoming an architect and being entrusted with rebuilding the capital were nothing more than the wishful daydreams of youth. If he was to avoid becoming another vagrant on the streets of Vienna, he needed inspiration and a keen sense of purpose. He was to find both that afternoon in the most unlikely of places.

The Hofburg Museum was a dull mausoleum dedicated to the past glories of the Hapsburg dynasty which Hitler despised. As far as the future Führer was concerned, they symbolized the old, degenerate aristocracy who had denied their German origins. As the rain clouds opened, he reluctantly sought refuge among the relics of Austria's imperialist past. According to crypto-historian Trevor Ravenscroft, author of the highly questionable

*Having failed to get into the Academy of Fine Arts in Vienna, Hitler (right)
escaped his aimless existence by moving to Munich in 1913 and enlisting in a
Bavarian frontline unit when war broke out. He later won the Iron Cross.*

but often quoted *Spear of Destiny* (1972), Hitler paid scant attention to the exhibits as he walked through the musty, ill-lit galleries hung with dark oil paintings in ornate gold frames and lined with artefacts in glass cabinets. But in the *Schatzkammer*, or treasure house, he paused before a display of ancient relics known collectively as the *Reichskleinoden*, unaware of the significance of what he was looking at, so deep was he in his own thoughts. It was only when a tour guide began to address a party of foreign visitors that crowded around him that Hitler was awakened from his reverie.

> '... *their guide pointed to an ancient spearhead ... And then I heard the words which were to change my whole life: "There is a legend associated with this spear that whoever claims it, and solves its secrets, holds the destiny of the world in his hands for good or evil."*'

The spearhead, known officially as the Sword of St Maurice, was rumoured to be the Holy Lance or Spear of Longinus with which a Roman centurion had pierced the side of Jesus before he was taken down from the Cross after his crucifixion. For this reason, it was deemed to possess magical properties and was thereafter known as the Spear of Destiny. Charlemagne (742–814), the first Holy Roman Emperor, was said to have attributed his unbroken string of victories to his possession of the spear. He died shortly after it had fallen from his hand when his horse had reared and thrown him to the ground.

A similar fate befell the 12th-century German conqueror Frederick Barbarossa who dropped the spear while crossing a river in Asia Minor and was immediately struck down and killed. No fewer than 45 emperors carried the spear.

Considering its bloody and illustrious history, it appeared, at first glance, to be an unremarkable object. The rust-encrusted, leaf-shaped blade had been crudely repaired with wire and lay within an open leather case on a red velvet dais. Had it not been for the tiny crosses of gold embossed on the base, it would have been indistinguishable from hundreds of similar weapons of the period held by museums around the world. There was no proof that the relic on display in the Hofburg Museum was the genuine article, but that did not seem to deter Hitler who later claimed that he experienced a revelation when he first came into its presence. He later wrote:

> *'I knew with immediacy that this was an important moment in my life. And yet I could not divine why an outwardly Christian symbol should make such an impression upon me. I stood there quietly gazing upon it for several minutes quite oblivious to the scene in the* Schatzkammer *around me. It seemed to carry some hidden inner meaning which evaded me, a meaning which I felt I inwardly knew yet could not bring to consciousness … The spear appeared to be some sort of magical medium of revelation for it brought the world of ideas into such close and living perspective that human imagination became more real than the world of sense.*

'I felt as though I myself had held it in my hands before in some earlier century of history – that I myself had once claimed it as my talisman of power and held the destiny of the world in my hands. Yet how could this be possible? What sort of madness was this that was invading my mind and creating such turmoil in my breast?'

Whether the spear was the genuine article or not is almost irrelevant. Clearly, Hitler had awakened something within himself which was to empower him with a sense of his own destiny and infallibility.

HITLER TRACES THE HISTORY OF THE SPEAR

The following morning Hitler visited the Hof Library to learn as much as he could about the spear, its legend and its history. Although he was too indolent to read anything other than magazines and *Schnulzenromane* (sentimental novels) in adulthood, he had apparently been an avid, if indiscriminate, reader in his youth, if his school friend August Kubizek is to be believed.

'Books were his whole world. In Vienna he used the Hof library so industriously that I asked him once, in all seriousness, whether he intended to read the whole library,

Frederick Barbarossa drops the Spear of Destiny on his way to the Third Crusade and meets his end in the river.

which, of course, earned some rude remarks. One day he took me along to the library and showed me the reading room. I was almost overwhelmed by the enormous masses of books and I asked him how it was he managed to get what he wanted. He began to explain to me the use of the various catalogues which confused me even more.'

To his dismay, Hitler discovered that numerous conquerors had claimed to possess the *Heilige,* or Victory Lance, concurrently through the centuries and that there was no certain way of proving whether the artefact in the *Schatzkammer* was authentic. The first written reference to the Hofburg spear appeared in the ancient *Anglo-Saxon Chronicle* recording the Battle of Leck in which Otto the Great triumphed over the Mongols, but prior to this its origins were unknown.

According to crypto-historian, Trevor Ravenscroft, in *The Spear of Destiny*, Hitler returned later that afternoon to the *Schatzkammer* for a second look at the object that now completely obsessed him.

'I slowly became aware of a mighty presence around it – the same awesome presence which I had experienced inwardly on those rare occasions in my life when I had sensed that a great destiny awaited me.'

Ravenscroft fails to provide a source for these quotations and one is forced to ask if this melodramatic scene, and perhaps the bulk of the book, is purely speculative fiction. However, let us assume for the moment that this account has some basis in fact, as the author claimed. In his altered state of awareness, Hitler is said to have been privileged to the realization that the spear was a portal between the worlds of spirit and matter.

> 'The air became stifling so that I could barely breathe. The noisy scene of the Treasure House seemed to melt away before my eyes. I stood alone and trembling before the hovering form of the Superman [Übermensch] – a Spirit sublime and fearful, a countenance intrepid and cruel. In holy awe, I offered my soul as a vessel of his Will ...'

And then came the vision which decided his destiny.

> 'A *window in the future was opened up to me through which I saw in a single flash of illumination, a future event by which I knew beyond contradiction that the blood in my veins would one day become the vessel of the folk-spirit of my people.*'

It is thought that the revelation Hitler referred to was a vision of the future in which he saw himself entering Vienna in triumph on the day Austria was assimilated into the Reich on 12 March 1938. In a speech before the ecstatic crowds celebrating the *Anschluss* in the Austrian capital he appeared to refer to that same vision when he said: 'Providence has charged me with a mission to reunite the German Peoples ... I have lived for it and I believe I have now fulfilled it.' And it was on that day that he ordered the removal of the Hapsburg regalia to Germany aboard an armoured train.

ENTER DR STEIN

The source for these intimate episodes was not Hermann Rauschning, the minor Nazi official who it is alleged fraudulently claimed to have been privy to Hitler's innermost thoughts, leading several generations of historians astray, but an even more inconspicuous figure, Dr Walter Johannes Stein (1891–1957). Stein was a respected Viennese Doctor of Philosophy and anthroposophist (a follower of Rudolph Steiner), who was said to have been employed as a confidential advisor to Winston Churchill after fleeing Nazi-occupied Europe in 1933 in order to escape being pressed into service by Himmler's Occult Bureau. As with Louis de Wohl, the astrologer, Dr Stein was apparently considered to be of value to the British who were keen for inside knowledge on the Führer's mental state so that they could anticipate his future strategies, but were also curious to discover what occult methods the Nazis were employing to locate vulnerable Allied convoys.

According to Ravenscroft, the prime minister swore Stein to secrecy regarding the extent to which the British used psychics in spying and self-defence, but in the summer of 1957 Stein decided that he had kept the secret long enough and that it was time to tell the truth. Three days later he collapsed and he died soon afterwards. Fortunately for Ravenscroft, Stein had earlier confided in him after the author had initially sought out the academic on a matter of mutual interest, the Holy Grail. But with Stein silenced, there is now no way of corroborating Ravenscroft's account of Hitler's mystical experiences or the part Stein may have played in Britain's psychic self-defence. That said, it is worth repeating, for truth is often stranger than fiction.

THE FACE AT THE WINDOW

'The Beast does not look what he is. He may even have a comic moustache.'
Vladimir Soloviev, *A Story of the Antichrist* (1900)

In the summer of 1912, Walter Stein was starting his second term at Vienna University where he was studying for a science doctorate. It was an intensive course and Stein had to ration his free time. When he found he could afford to take a break he would spend it browsing through the musty antiquarian bookshops in the old quarter of the city near the banks of the Danube. At the back of one ill-lit shop, he is said to have chanced upon an annotated leather-bound copy of Wolfram von Eschenbach's epic prose poem, *Parzival*, annotated with insights and comments by someone who evidently had a thorough knowledge of their subject and more than a passing acquaintance with occult philosophy. Stein had been searching for a copy of the book ever since his parents had taken him to see Wagner's opera based on the same medieval legend of the knight's search for the Holy Grail. His researches had led him to conclude that the medieval Grail romance was based on historical figures of the 9th century and that the Holy Lance was not symbolic but an actual physical relic. So the book was a real find. He gladly paid the asking price and left the shop eager to examine his treasure.

A few streets further on, he took a window seat at Demel's fashionable café with a view of the Kohlmarkt and read the slender book from cover to cover in a single sitting. It became evident that the author of the hastily scrawled commentary had discovered a key to deciphering the secrets of the Grail legend encoded in the knight's quest. But while more enlightened readers would be likely to interpret the stages of the quest as trials of initiation, the previous owner had taken it as a confirmation of his belief in the superiority of the Aryan race. The marginalia revealed that their author despised the Christian ideal and possessed 'a working knowledge of the black arts'. By the time Stein closed the book, we are told, he realized he had been 'reading the footnotes of Satan!'

Little did Stein suspect that within the hour he would come face to face with its diabolical author. In a moment more contrived than a scene from a Mills & Boon romantic novel we are asked to believe that Stein then looked up from his book to gaze into the face of its starving wild-eyed author looking hungrily through the window at the rich Viennese gorging themselves on cream cakes and coffee!

Longinus pierces the side of the crucified Jesus with his spear, creating the holiest of Christian relics.

Hitler was dressed in a greasy, threadbare black overcoat several sizes too large and frayed trousers. His toes could be seen poking through the cracks in his shoes like a caricature of Charlie Chaplin. In fact, one suspects that Chaplin provided Ravenscroft with the inspiration for this tragicomic scene rather than Stein. When Stein left the café, the vagrant with the grizzled hair and comical moustache was still lingering in the Kohlmarkt selling his postcard-sized watercolours. On impulse Stein pressed a handful of marks into the artist's hand and accepted three sketches unseen before making his way back to his lodgings. There he laid them out beside the book that had so engrossed him in the café. It was only then that Stein noticed that the subject of one of the watercolours was the Heilige Lance as pictured on display in the Hofburg. Then he saw something which made the hair on the nape of his neck stand up. The signature of the artist and the name of the previous owner of the annotated *Parzival* were one and the same – Adolf Hitler.

Quite apart from the ludicrously contrived coincidences which characterize Ravenscroft's account, there are a number of factual anomalies which raise serious doubts as to the veracity of the events recorded in *The Spear of Destiny*. For example, when Dr Stein inquired where he might find Hitler, the bookseller mentioned that he had left Vienna to claim an inheritance from a recently deceased aunt. This was purportedly in the summer of 1912, but the only recently deceased aunt in the family was Johanna Polzl who had died the previous spring. Secondly, recent research has failed to find evidence of either

Ernst Pretzsche or his shop which one would expect to have been preserved in the city's meticulously kept archive, although there is the possibility that these records might have been destroyed in the war. But more significantly, doubts have been raised by the suspicious similarities between Ravenscroft's account of Steiner's discovery of the annotated *Parzival* pamphlet and an almost identical episode in Sir Edward Bulwer-Lytton's occult novel *Zanoni* (1842), which raises the question of whether Ravenscroft was 'inspired' by the novel, or whether it is simply an uncanny coincidence. And then there is the highly dubious presumption that someone who had annotated a book with personal comments and clues as to the work's true meaning would have been foolish enough to part with it in the first place! Most curious of all, though, is the fact that we are asked to believe that Dr Stein, a well educated, middle-class Jew, sought out a rabid anti-Semite – whose hatred of Jews was evident from his 'crude, vulgar and in many cases, obscene' handwritten comments in the margins of *Parzival* – even allowing for the unlikely possibility that he was desperate to share his passion for the Grail legend with a fellow 'seeker'.

These doubts in themselves do not of course automatically discredit the story, but once seemingly serious flaws such as these are identified the whole edifice begins to look decidedly unsound. And then there is the assertion made recently by German journalist Christoph Lindenberg in *Die Drie*, who found several significant inconsistencies in Ravenscroft's account and who states: 'At no time of life did Hitler live in impoverished conditions, rather he always had sufficient money. In the Meldenmann Strasse, a kind of large hotel, Hitler paid a rent of 15 kronen a month. So he could afford a fairly expensive room and had no need to sell his pictures.' However, let's give Ravenscroft the benefit of the doubt and see how far he asks us to suspend our disbelief.

IN SEARCH OF HITLER

In the following days, we are told, Stein went in search of the itinerant artist but could find no trace of him. Eventually he returned to Ernst Pretzsche's bookshop and asked the proprietor if he could supply Hitler's address. Pretzsche, an odious, balding, toad-like man, informed him that Hitler had not been in for more than three weeks, but he believed that he frequently stayed at a hostelry in Meldenmann Strasse. Seeing how eager the young student was to learn more about the author of the marginalia, Pretzsche invited him to step into a small back room. There he told Stein how he would occasionally cook for Hitler who was always in need of food, but was too proud to accept money. Hitler would pawn his books when he was truly desperate and Pretzsche would pay a few hellers to save him from sleeping in the street.

This is the myth Hitler created for himself and which others were to embellish; the impoverished future Führer, the misunderstood messiah suffering indignities and physical hardship for his people in the backstreets of Vienna. It is a fabricated self-image symptomatic of a neurotic paranoid

A watercolour of Munich's Odeonsplatz by the young and highly unsuccessful artist, Adolf Hitler. He described himself as an 'artist' until 1920, at which point he began calling himself a 'writer'.

personality which seeks to justify feelings of fear and rage by assuming the role of victim in order to have others rush to the rescue and offer reassurance. One can imagine Hitler learning the role from his doting mother to whom he fled whenever his authoritarian father became abusive. The truth of the Vienna years was far more mundane. Recent research suggests that Hitler never saw the inside of a flophouse, nor did he share a bug-infested apartment with his school friend Kubizek. An inheritance from his aunt Johanna Polzl and his father's modest civil service pension allowed him to live in comparative comfort during these 'missing years', which he spent lying in bed until mid-morning just as he was later to do at Berchtesgaden, then venturing out to sell his watercolours in clothes that may not have been tailor-made, but were of sufficient quality at least to give the lie to the image of the emaciated Viennese vagrant.

So zealously did Hitler preserve this mythologized self-image that he even risked alienating his supporters in the early years of the party. Some were so incensed by their leader's pathological need for secrecy that they circulated a leaflet among the members expressing their concerns, including their suspicion that he was sponsored by silent partners who desired to dictate party policy.

> 'He regards the time as ripe for bringing dissension and schism into our ranks by means of the shadowy people behind him … It grows more and more clear that his purpose is simply to use the National Socialist Party for his own immoral purposes. A further point is the question of his occupation and finances. If ever individual members enquire what he actually lives on and what his previous occupation has been, he always gets excited and loses his temper.'

Konrad Heiden, a Munich journalist and author of *The History of National Socialism* (1932) and *Birth of the Third Reich* (1934), noted: 'The man is by nature secretive, his life does not lie open to his friends. Questions regarding his private affairs offend him.' Unsettled and embarrassed by intellectually superior people and those who were not afraid to speak their minds, Hitler would start ranting in an effort to disguise the paucity of his argument or relapse into a sullen sulk.

When detailing Stein's second visit to the bookshop in Vienna, Ravenscroft describes Pretzsche pointing out a pile of books that Hitler had pawned, including works by Hegel, Schopenhauer and Nietzsche. But again, there is no proof that this event ever took place, and considerable reliable testimony to suggest that it did not. As has already been noted, Hitler had no interest in serious literature. Those who knew him personally have stated that he would re-read the same adolescent adventure stories over and over and was even given to quoting passages to impress guests to the Reichs Chancellery and at Berchtesgaden. His favourite novels were those by Karl May, the author of a series of Native American adventure stories in the Fennimore Cooper vein and a series of books concerning the *schmaltzig* adventures of a horse called Raubautz. Presumably, he resisted the temptation to recite these from memory when entertaining educated foreign dignitaries. When table talk tired him, he would indulge his petit bourgeois taste in entertainment with frivolous romantic film comedies provided by the ever-obliging Goebbels. Such a picture is clearly in stark contrast to Ravenscroft's image of the feverishly intellectual novice magician poring over the world's wealth of occult philosophy.

If there is any doubt as to which is the truer picture, it should be noted that Hitler's private secretary, Christa Schroeder, affirmed, 'His library contained no classic and no single book of humane or intellectual value.' Meanwhile, Hitler himself admitted to his intellectual limitations when he said, 'I read to confirm my ideas.'

Even his school friend Kubizek, who had given such a heroic image of the young Hitler at the Hof Library, later admitted in a private letter to the Linz archivist, Franz Jetzinger, that there were only two books that Hitler had actually read with enthusiasm: a child's guide to Nordic mythology and a history of German archaeology in which he had discovered the symbol that was to cast its shadow over Europe – the swastika.

INFERNAL INITIATION

Ravenscroft's *Spear of Destiny* appears to belong to the same literary genre that gave rise to *The Da Vinci Code* (2003), works of highly speculative fiction featuring historical characters. As such we have to take the following events he describes in Pretzsche's shop as a possible, if unlikely, scenario rather than as historical fact.

While the proprietor probed Stein for personal details and his political sympathies, the student surveyed the chaotically cramped room which served as Pretzsche's office. He noted a number of prints illustrating alchemical processes and astrological charts alongside anti-Semitic cartoons of a pornographic nature. While Pretzsche pressed his question, Stein studied a group photograph on the desk in which his interrogator was shown beside Guido von List, the pan-German mystic who had been accused of practising satanic sexual magic and who Ravenscroft falsely alleged had been run out of Vienna by an outraged populace. In truth, von List was a dreamer, an armchair Armanist who advocated a return to nature and the worship of Wotan. He was obsessed with the occult significance of runic symbols and wrote long, learned treatises on the subject which were a profound influence on Himmler, but he was no Aleister Crowley.

Pretzsche however considered himself an adept of the dark arts and offered to initiate Stein into the arcane mysteries. 'I am considered in some quarters to be a great authority on occultism,' he is said to have boasted. 'Adolf Hitler is not the only person to whom I give assistance and advice in these matters.'

Firmly but politely refusing the offer, Stein hurried out of the shop and made his way to the hostelry where he was informed that Herr Hitler had left the city to claim a small inheritance from an aunt who had died at Spittal-an-der-Drau. The manager did not expect Hitler to return.

It was to be another ten days before Stein happened to see Hitler painting outside the Hofburg and noted the remarkable improvement in his appearance. Hitler resisted the stranger's awkward attempt to engage in conversation. He didn't seek approval for his art and nor was he moved by a young student's assertion that they shared a common interest in the spear. Not, that is, until Stein mentioned that he, too, had unearthed proof from a German chronicle in Cologne that the Holy Lance was of Teutonic origin. Hitler's eyes blazed into life. Little did he suspect that his fellow enthusiast with his classic Aryan looks was actually a Jew.

Poet, rower, businessman and reader of the runes, Guido 'von' List (1848–1919), founder of the Ariosophical Society.

Together they entered the *Schatzkammer* and stood before the display case in which the spear was housed, lost in contemplation. Stein, we are asked to believe, was overcome with a vision of the crucified Christ in the presence of this sacred Christian relic, while his unlikely companion became possessed by its promise of power.

'Hitler stood beside him like a man in a trance,' writes Ravenscroft, 'a man over whom some dreadful magic spell had been cast. His face was flushed and his brooding eyes shone with an alien emanation.' Stein became aware that the spear was radiating a 'ghostly ectoplasmic light' which Hitler absorbed into the core of his being.

The transformation was terrifying. Stein feared he was witnessing Hitler's possession by the Antichrist, though Ravenscroft fails to explain how a Christian relic could attract satanic forces.

HITLER'S SATANIC INITIATION

The lance, we are told, acted like a divining rod for the dark forces which are continually seeking entry into our world of matter. In the summer of 1912, Adolf Hitler was clearly ready to submit to its influence. Why then did he continue to behave like an impotent, hysterical neurotic even after he had enlisted in the army in 1914 when his dark star ought surely to have been in the ascendant? Despite his claim to have finally answered his true calling, he acted so erratically that his comrades kept their distance and his superiors repeatedly passed him over for promotion because they knew the men would refuse to follow him. As fellow soldier Hans Mend later recalled:

> '[Hitler was considered] *a peculiar fellow. He sat in the corner of our mess holding his head in his hands in deep concentration. Suddenly, he would leap up and, running about excitedly, say that in spite of all our efforts victory would be denied us, for the invisible foes of the German people were a greater danger than the biggest cannon of the enemy. On other occasions, he sat with his helmet pulled over his head quite oblivious to our world, buried so deeply within himself that none of us could arouse him … We all cursed him and found him intolerable. There was this white crow among us that did not go along with us when we damned the war.'*

Were these the actions of the Antichrist or the devil's disciple? If so, Satan had made a very poor choice. Moreover, if Hitler was the all-powerful instrument of such diabolical force, why did it take more than 20 years for him to claw his way to the Chancellorship? There can be no doubt that Hitler was possessed – those who witnessed his powers to whip up a mob attested to that fact – but he was driven by demons of this world, not the next. They were the demons of resentment, fear, self-loathing and all-consuming hatred. The fact is, Hitler didn't need help from the dark side. He had enough destructive energy within him to wreak havoc on a scale unimaginable even in the days of Vlad the Impaler, Tamburlaine and Genghis Khan.

The year before Stein witnessed the terrible transformation in the *Schatzkammer*, Hitler, it is said, had begun the process of initiation which would culminate in his possession by the spear. With Pretzsche as his mentor, the 22-year-old Hitler was introduced to the esoteric mysteries of alchemy and the significance of the symbolism encoded in the Grail legend. But his was not to be the path of patience and self-discipline leading ultimately to self-realization and enlightenment, but the perilous short-cut through the use of a narcotic stimulant, peyotl, whose active principle was mescalin, the drug of choice favoured by the high priests of sex magick such as Aleister Crowley.

ADOLF IN WONDERLAND

In Ravenscroft's version of events, the final act in Hitler's Faustian pact with Lucifer takes on all the characteristics of a Grimm fairy tale as he describes young Adolf venturing into the forest of Wachau near Vienna with Stein by his side in search of the *Waldschrat* (forest troll) who had introduced him to the pleasures of peyotl.

It was the spring of 1913, the last idyllic spring before the outbreak of the Great War, and Hitler had decided to say goodbye to an old friend, Hans Lodz, before he left to try his luck in Munich. Lodz was a herbalist who lived in a cabin in the country. Two years earlier, he had literally stumbled upon Hitler who had been sleeping rough in the woods and invited him back to his rustic home where he prepared a witches' brew from the peyotl roots that Pretzsche had provided. Now Lodz greeted him again as a master would a favoured pupil, his eyes glinting with pride through flowing white hair, a grin creasing the features of his gnarled, bark-like skin. While Lodz cooked a vegetable broth, Hitler detailed his experiences with the mind-expanding hallucinogen to his young companion. Stein sat attentively as Hitler described the shock at finding himself adrift in the dream-like landscape of his own psyche where every aspiration and anxiety could take on symbolic form. One can only wonder what sights and sensations manifested in the mind of such a man, on the brink of starvation, half-crazed with delusions of grandeur and suffering from persecution mania, but we have the personal accounts of several aspiring mystics to give a hint of what the young Hitler might have experienced, assuming, of course, that this event actually took place.

THE DOORS OF PERCEPTION

In May 1953, the British novelist, Aldous Huxley, ingested a small quantity of mescalin in the hope that it might grant him a glimpse of 'the ultimate reality' and reveal the meaning behind the apparently random chaos of existence. Huxley had been assured by the Californian scientists who monitored this experiment that there would be no side effects as the drug was derived from peyotl, a natural hallucinogen found in the cactus plant peyote, which the Native American shamans had been using for centuries to attain altered states of consciousness.

'I had expected to lie with my eyes shut, looking at visions of many coloured geometries, of animated architectures, rich with gems and fabulously lovely, of landscapes with heroic figures, of symbolic dramas trembling perpetually on the verge of the ultimate revelation. But I had not reckoned, it was evident, with the idiosyncrasies of my mental make-up, the facts of my temperament, training and habits.'

What was going on in Adolf Hitler's mind? A remarkable photograph from August 1914 shows him among the crowd in Munich's Odeonsplatz when war was declared, but this photo is almost certainly a fake.

To Huxley's astonishment, the very fabric of the physical world appeared to be alive. Everything, from a vase of flowers to the creases in his trousers, became objects of awe, illuminated from within and infinitely interesting.

> *'A bunch of flowers shining with their own inner light ... Those folds – what a labyrinth of endless significant complexity! ... I was seeing what Adam had seen on the morning of his own creation – the miracle, moment by moment, of naked existence.'*

Whether Hitler shared a similar experience or whether, as seems more likely, he endured a 'bad trip' due to his neurotic psychological state no one knows. But he is said to have confided one startling insight from his drug-induced vision to Stein on this, their final evening together.

Hitler boasted that he had unwittingly tapped into that matrix of memories and mental impressions in the ether known in esoteric circles as the Akashic Record. There he glimpsed images of his past lives passing before his inner eye like frames in a cinema film.

One of them was Landulf of Capua, the historical inspiration for the central character in Wagner's opera *Parsifal*, but he was not the opera's hero. He was its villain, Klingsor, the embodiment of evil.

TABLE TALK

Cynics will doubtless revel in the absurdity of the above scene, but it is worth noting that Hitler's reputed drug habit was common knowledge among eminent occultists during the dictator's lifetime. The English poet and theosophist, Victor Neuburg, once wrote an account of an after-dinner discussion with Aleister Crowley and Aldous Huxley in Neuburg's Berlin apartment in 1938 during which they touched on the subject.

> *"You know Hitler has taken the stuff [mescalin]," Crowley observed. "I heard it from a reliable friend in the OTO."*
>
> *"OTO?" inquired Huxley.*
>
> *"The Ordo Templi Orientis. [The Ordo Templi Orientis, founded by Theodor Reuss, Franz Hartmann and Carl Kellner in 1895, promoted the practice of sex magick and is not to be confused with the more influential Order of the New Templars founded by Lanz Liebenfels.] My local branch, you might say. And their connections with the Nazis are nobody's business. They almost founded the party, or at least subverted it. Do you know that two of their chief men personally trained Adolf Hitler? Before, he was a stuttering Austrian oaf, a shoddy Bohemian and a pervert to boot. They taught him oratory, rhetoric and, under the influence of this drug that will shortly, my dear Aldous, set your eyes on fire, gave him his daemon."*
>
> *"Then," Huxley said, "all the disparate romanticism that, in its waning, found expression in the irrational,*

in secret cults, has made its kingdom here. Fascism, is, after all, the triumph of decadence, the final madness of Bohemia."

"So that carnage of Ahriman may be complete, precisely" Crowley replied.'

But, again, there are those who doubt that such a conversation ever took place. They state categorically that Neuburg and Crowley ended their friendship in 1914 and point to Crowley's diaries which record the meeting with Aldous Huxley in Berlin as being on Saturday, 4 October 1930, not 1938. Despite these discrepancies, it is almost certain Crowley was responsible for introducing Huxley to mescalin. Hitler, however, probably never took peyotl in his life, although he was certainly fatally crippled by his addiction to prescription drugs in the last year of the war, thanks to his quack physician, Dr Theodor Morell.

SÉANCE ON A WET AFTERNOON

'No words of mine can describe the satisfaction I felt ... I am not ashamed to say that, carried away by the emotion of the moment, I sank down on my knees and thanked heaven in the fullness of my heart for the favour of having been permitted to live at such a time.'

Hitler (on receiving his call-up papers in
August 1914), *Mein Kampf*

Ravenscroft's re-imagining of history returns to a remotely recognizable reality with Hitler's ecstatic reaction to the declaration of war in 1914 and his experiences in the trenches for which he was awarded the Iron Cross First Class. But at the war's end, the facts once more are enshrouded in myth as the principal players in this supernatural melodrama reassemble to renew their Faustian pact in a scene worthy of pulp horror writer, H. P. Lovecraft.

The year is 1919 and members of a sinister occult brotherhood are holding a séance in Munich in the hope of making contact with their 'Hidden Masters' on the higher planes of existence.

They call themselves the *Thule Gesellschaft* (after a legendary prehistoric Nordic civilization) and comprise leading members of the community including judges, police chiefs, university professors, industrialists, army officers and the aristocracy. All have sworn to rid Germany of Zionist influence and to promote German nationalism, by violent means if necessary. They are led by a fiercely anti-Semitic, middle-aged Bavarian journalist named Dietrich Eckart who is destined to be the mentor to Adolf Hitler and the future editor-in-chief of the official Nazi newspaper, the *Völkischer Beobachter* [People's Observer]. Eckart's frustrated ambitions to be a playwright led him to alcoholism, morphine addiction and a stay in a mental asylum. He thought of himself as an intellectual, but he betrayed his true nature when he told a gathering in the Brennessel Wine Cellar that spring:

> 'We need a man at the head who can stand the sound of a machine gun. The rabble need to get fear in their pants.

The Thule Gesellschaft *were fanatical nationalists, and held meetings in Munich's Four Seasons Hotel.*

*We can't use an officer because people don't respect them
anymore. The best man for the job would be a worker who
knows how to talk … He doesn't need much brains … He
must be a bachelor, then we'll get the women.'*

On the evening of their séance he is joined by two émigré
Polish generals with an interest in spiritualism and a strong
sympathy for the German nationalist cause, Generals
Skoropadski and Bishupski. Seated with them around the
table in the darkened room is the founder of the group, Rudolf
Glauer, the future editor of the group's publications, Conrad
Ritzler and Eckart's protégé, German-Russian refugee Alfred
Rosenberg (1893–1946), who was to become a formative
influence on Nazi racist ideology.

Although the Thule Society was not a magical order in
the mould of the Golden Dawn, the members shared their
counterpart's fascination with paranormal phenomena, their
obsession with secrecy and their practice of creating exotic
histories for themselves. Glauer, for example, insisted on being
addressed as Count Heinrich von Sebottendorf, although in reality
he was the working-class son of a Dresden engine driver. He also
professed a profound knowledge of esoteric lore and muttered
unintelligibly about having been initiated into 'the Mysteries'
during a sojourn in Turkey, but in truth he had merely digested
passages from the Theosophist sacred text, *The Secret Doctrine*
(1888), and regurgitated it with Germanic embellishments. The
three-volume treatise on the origin and nature of the universe had

been 'channelled' by the eccentric medium Madame Blavatsky and contained the germ of an idea that the Nazis were to expand upon and pervert for their own ends – this was the myth of the Master Race. Glauer simply appropriated Blavatsky's cosmology and her concept of the Seven Root Races of Man for German consumption, claiming that it proved that the ancient Edda legends on which Wagner based his *Ring* Cycle had a basis in fact. Rosenberg was to go one stage further in his racist revisionist history *The Myth of the Twentieth Century* (1930) in which he claimed that the superior Aryan race had originated on the lost continent of Atlantis from where its ships sailed forth to found the earliest centres of civilization. But on the night of the séance, these men had something other than politics on their mind.

While they looked on in hushed expectation, the naked medium, a ruddy-faced, muscular Russian farmer's wife, sank into a deep trance to allow herself to be taken over by her spirit guides. It was their voices which now issued from her throat, each distinctive and talking in its mother tongue of which their host had no knowledge. It was an impressive performance, more convincing even than the manifestations of gossamer-white ectoplasm which she usually produced. Glauer lost his nerve and attempted to break free of the circle, but Eckart restrained him. It was then that the ghostly apparition of a former member of the group formed in their midst. They all recognized it as Prince von Thurn und Taxis who had been murdered only months before. His voice was also unmistakable. In High German, a version of the language with which the Russian peasant woman was unfamiliar, the disembodied head of the prince declared that the new leader of Germany would claim the Holy Lance and embark on a campaign of world conquest. A moment later his form faded back into the darkness and was replaced by another disincarnate spirit – that of the Countess von Westarp. She too had been an active member of the group before she was murdered by communists. She had returned to announce the imminent arrival of the messiah for whom they had been waiting so long. But she added a warning that their new leader would be exposed as a false prophet and would drag the nation into the abyss.

With a sharp intake of breath, the medium awoke from her trance and the apparitions disappeared. No one moved or spoke for several minutes.

HITLER TAKES THE STAGE

'Where he comes from, no one can say. From a prince's palace perhaps, or a day labourer's cottage. But everyone knows: he is the Führer, everyone cheers him and thus one day he will present himself, he for all of us are waiting, full of longing, who feel Germans present distress deep in our hearts, so that thousands and hundreds of thousands of brains picture him, millions of voices call for him, one single German soul seeks him.'

Kurt Hesse (1922), from Joachim Fest's
Face of the Third Reich (1972)

While Eckart and his co-subversives were groping in the dark for a sign of their future saviour, Adolf Hitler was standing in the shadows in a backroom at the Alte Rosenbad tavern in the Herrenstrasse observing a group of backstreet radicals arguing over their lack of funds.

It was the evening of the 13 September 1919 and he had been sent there to report on their activities by his army paymasters who were looking for an organization that they could infiltrate and manipulate for their own ends – namely, to counter the growing tide of anti-Nationalist sentiment among the working class. Hitler had witnessed an earlier meeting of the German Workers' Party or DAP (the predecessor of the Nazi Party), which at the time had fewer than 60 members and he had not been impressed by the quality of the debate or the views expressed by its guest speaker, a Bavarian nationalist academic. In fact, he had returned merely to inform the committee that he had decided not to join their 'absurd little organization'.

Those who are tempted to romanticize Nazism would do well to remember the nature of the personalities who attended that fateful meeting, one of whom was Doktor Wilhelm Gutberlet, who swore by the efficacy of his sidereal pendulum which he claimed could locate any Jew in a crowded room. 'Hitler availed himself of Gutberlet's mystic powers,' recalled an aide, 'and had many discussions with him on the racial question.' Such was the character of the men who were to guide the destiny of a nation.

Hitler later recalled that early meeting in *Mein Kampf*:

'In the grim light of a tiny gas lamp four people were sitting at a table and they once greeted me as a member of the German Workers' Party. The minutes of the last meeting were read and the secretary gave a vote of confidence. Next came the treasury report – all in all the party possessed seven marks and fifty pfennigs – for which the treasurer received a vote of confidence. This too was entered into the minutes ... Terrible, terrible! This was club life of the worst sort. Was I to join such an organisation?'

Returning to his barracks he considered his future which looked bleak in the extreme.

'That I was poor and without means seemed to me the most bearable part of it, but it was harder that I was numbered among the nameless, that I was one of the millions whom chance permits to live or summoned out of existence without even their closest neighbours condescending to take any notice of it. In addition, there was the difficulty which inevitably arose from my lack of schooling. After two days of agonised pondering and reflection, I finally came to the conviction that I had to take this step.'

The air of self-pity is positively suffocating.

THE MUNICH MYTH

Such was the personal myth Hitler was intent on creating, although, in fact, he had no choice in the matter. He had been ordered to take charge of the fledgling party by Army Intelligence who promised him practically unlimited financial backing and a loyal intake of new members who were all under orders to join.

With the financial backing of the army and a hired audience to applaud his speeches, Hitler's confidence as a public speaker grew in tandem with the party's fortunes. Reports of his early speeches reveal that he was yet to demonstrate the charismatic, demonstrative style that was to draw the slavering masses, but the major themes were already in evidence – a pathological hatred of the Jews and a belief that they had stabbed Germany in the back to end the war prematurely. A contemporary journalist wrote:

> 'The lecturer [Hitler] gave a talk on Jewry, showing that wherever one looks, one sees Jews. The whole of Germany is governed by Jews. It is a scandal that the German workers, whether with hand or brain, let themselves be exploited by the Jews because the Jews have money. The Jewish swindlers dominate the government. When the Jew has filled his pockets at the public till he drives the poor German worker into confusion, thus keeping himself in control of things. The lecturer also spoke about Russia and the responsibility for what happened there [the

October Revolution]. *The Jews had made the revolution. Therefore Germans must unite and fight against the Jews or they would gobble up the last crumbs from the national table. The lecturer's concluding words were: "We shall carry on the struggle until the last Jew has been removed from the Reich – even if it comes to an insurrection or even revolution." The lecturer received great applause.'*

Inevitably, such diatribes attracted the attention of Dietrich Eckart and his Thulist nationalists, who, unknown to Hitler, were the puppet-masters behind the party they had created to serve their nationalist ambitions. When Eckart witnessed Hitler in action, he knew immediately that he had found his messiah and that pretty soon the nominal head of the DAP, railway engineer Anton Drexler, and his co-founder, Karl Harrer, would be forced to concede control to their latest recruit. 'Here is the one for whom I was but the prophet and the forerunner,' Eckart declared alluding to John the Baptist and Jesus of Nazareth.

Hitler was apparently equally enthusiastic, seeing in Eckart a man who could be both his mentor and his spiritual brother. 'This Dietrich Eckart is a man I can admire,' Hitler told a friend. 'He appears to know the meaning of hatred and how to apply it.'

He was referring to Eckart's gangster tactics in disrupting the commemoration for a murdered communist by having bags of 'bitches' blood' thrown at posters of the dead man to attract the attention of the city's male dog population who would urinate on them. It was alleged that the assassin was none other than Eckart himself.

A 'MAD LITTLE CLOWN'

Presumably, these extracurricular activities were unknown to the playwright's patrons: the bankers, businessmen and intellectuals of Bavarian high society to whom he eagerly introduced the somewhat dishevelled Austrian corporal over the course of the following months. Some of Eckart's gilt-edged friends were condescending, others merely curious, as they remarked on the striking resemblance between Hitler and the most famous screen comedian of the period, Charlie Chaplin. (Even Mussolini was to comment on the similarity when he referred to Hitler as 'a mad little clown'.) Some must have wondered if this was a practical joke. Few were genuinely impressed by their friend's latest protégé, but they willingly agreed to contribute to the anti-Jewish crusade. In return each was promised whatever the cunning political agitator guessed they wanted to hear – a guarantee of lower interest rates, a pledge to disband the unions, a promise to return to traditional family values and so on. Even the intellectuals were not immune to Nazi charm.

Perhaps it was the frisson of being in proximity to danger (or primal power) which attracted them. Some fled abroad while there was still time. Others, such as the writer Hans Heinz Ewers, succumbed completely. Ewers, who went on to write the Nazi anthem, the 'Horst Wessel' song, was under no illusions as to the nature of the party he had joined, sensing in it 'the strongest expression of the powers of darkness'. Those who remained spellbound by the power and pageantry must have had a rude awakening on 10 May 1933 when the Nazis burned the books of writers whose ideas they feared in 30 cities across the Reich. Those intellectuals who had flirted with fascism should have recalled the words of the poet Heinrich Heine who warned in 1823: 'When they burn books, they will too in the end burn people.' Such rites were the clearest evidence yet that Nazism was not a political movement but a satanic cult in the true sense of the word. The Party gained strength by exploiting the primitive human instinct to destroy what we fear because we do not understand it and cannot control it.

Ten years earlier, Hitler was already on the road to power and his popularity was gathering momentum. It was only a matter of time before socio-economic factors created conditions sufficiently favourable for his accession.

Eckart did not live to see Hitler seize power. In the autumn of 1923 he lay dying, burnt out by a life of addiction to alcohol and morphine. With his last breath, he invoked the old gods through his treasured 'Mecca Stone', a black meteorite which he believed served as a portal between the worlds of spirit and matter. His last words were reputed to be: 'Follow Hitler. He will dance, but it is I who have called the tune. I have initiated him into the Secret Doctrine, opened his centres of vision and given him the means to communicate with the Powers. Do not mourn me for I shall have influenced history more than any other German.'

AN UNHOLY TRINITY

'Beware, you dogs. When the Devil is loose in me you will not curb him again.'

Joseph Goebbels

When Hitler's reputation as a public speaker grew during the early 1920s, he began to attract kindred spirits who believed Destiny had led them to the man who would restore Germany to its former glory. Rudolph Hess and Martin Bormann were typical of the fawning, anonymous 'yes men' with whom Hitler surrounded himself, but the real inner circle who took an active role in influencing policy and determining who would live and who would die were Himmler, Goering and Goebbels.

The first of this unholy trinity to pledge allegiance was the man his rivals called 'the poison dwarf'. Joseph Goebbels first heard Hitler speak at a party debate in Bamberg and had been so swayed by the strength of his leader's argument that he immediately conceded defeat, swearing undying loyalty before the meeting was closed – the first and last time the future 'Minister of Misinformation' would admit to being wrong on any matter in public.

Goebbels was the arch-propagandist of the Nazi regime, but it seems he also possessed a gift for prophecy. On one occasion, and only one, he had foreseen his first fateful meeting with his future Führer, which was to prove uncannily similar to the scene as it was to unfold in real life. It was in the summer of 1918 and Goebbels was then a student at the University of Freiburg. He made his prediction in a novel called *Michael* in which the idealistic young hero despairs of ridding his fatherland of Jewish influence until he meets a messianic saviour whose power of oratory awakens the sleeping nation. We can assume its author shared his hero's emotions on hearing Hitler speak for the first time.

'... *all of a sudden, the flow of his speech is unleashed ... I am captivated. Honour! Work! The Flag! Are there still such things in this people from whom God has taken His blessing hand.*

'*The audience is aglow. Hopes shine on grey faces. Someone clenches his fist. Another wipes the sweat off his brow. An old officer weeps like a child.*

'*I am getting hot and cold. I don't know what has happened to me ... And the man up there speaks on, and whatever was budding in me takes shape. A miracle! Those around me are no longer strangers. They are brothers. I approach the rostrum and look into the man's face. No orator he! But a prophet! Sweat is pouring down his face. A pair of eyes glow in the pale face. His fists are clenched. And like the last judgement, word after word is thundering on, phrase after phrase.*

'I do not know what to do. I seem demented. I begin to cheer and no one seems astonished. From the rostrum he glances at me for an instant. Those blue eyes sear me like a flame, this is a command.

'I feel like I am reborn. I know now where my path leads me. The path of destiny. I appear to be intoxicated. All I remember is the man's hand clasping mine. An oath for life and my eyes meet two large blue stars.'

Many years later, Goebbels recorded his initial impressions of the man to whom he was to devote his life and considerable energies.

'I thank fate that there is such a man! ... He is the creative instrument of fate and deity. I stand by him deeply shaken ... That is how it is ... I recognise him as my leader quite unconditionally ... He is so deep and mystical. He knows how to express infinite truth ... He seems like a prophet of old. And in the sky a big white cloud seems to take the shape of a swastika. Is this a sign of fate? How much elementary strength is there in this man compared to the intellectuals? On top of it all, his overwhelming personality ... With such a man one can conquer the world. To him I feel deeply linked. My doubts vanish ... I could not bear to have to doubt this man. Germany will live. Heil Hitler!'

Joseph Goebbels

'Hitler's words were spoken word for word as though from my own soul.'

Hermann Goering

It is unlikely that Hermann Goering shared Goebbels' idealistic image of Hitler as 'deep and mystical' or the instrument of 'infinite truth'. A former Great War fighter ace with the famous Richthofen squadron (whose comrades accused him of exaggerating his score of kills) and a strutting egotist of the first order, he considered himself second to no man – with the exception of his Führer. 'I have no conscience,' he once

'The poison dwarf': Goebbels was a key member of the inner circle with power over life and death.

declared. 'My conscience is Adolf Hitler.' But he saw Hitler as a leader, not as a mystic. 'I joined the party because I was a revolutionary,' he declared, 'not because of any ideological nonsense.' He had no beliefs other than the divine right of the aristocracy to rule and considered himself 'a Renaissance man', presumably in the mould of Cesare Borgia. He had a passion for good food, the finest cigars, hunting and fine art, but he despised 'culture', by which he meant anything that sought to educate or edify. This, if nothing else, he shared with Goebbels who had famously said, 'When I hear the word "culture", I reach for my revolver.'

Goering had grown up on a magnificent estate and was accustomed to getting his way in all things. His own mother had the measure of him when she predicted that he would either be a 'great man or a great criminal'. But he lacked purpose until he found it in the Führer. In return he acted as a stabilizing influence when Hitler succumbed to one of his periodic panic attacks. The fiercely aristocratic Goering was evidently in the thrall of the former corporal and curiously untroubled by the inequality in their backgrounds, but he was intimidated by Hitler's unpredictability and violent irrational outbursts. He admitted, 'In Hitler's presence, my heart would sink into my trousers.'

It was rumoured that Goering had a Jewish godfather with whom his mother had had an affair and it was this which embittered him towards Jews in general. In their efforts to portray him as the jovial lord of the manor, historians tend to forget that it was Goering, and not Himmler, who implemented the programme of concentration camp construction and it was also Goering who established the dreaded Gestapo. He relished his role as a genial avuncular figure, but it was a façade hiding a vicious and vindictive streak which could lash out at any moment. He celebrated his wedding by ordering an execution and kept a small black book in which he recorded the names of those he intended to eliminate at the next opportunity, giving rise to the saying, 'In any other country you have to justify having a gun; in Goering's Germany you have to justify why you don't use one.'

His aristocratic background and reputation as a war hero lent the party a respectability which helped to attract funding from influential industrialists and the nobility.

PURSUED BY DEMONS

'Hitler is an awakener of souls, the vehicle of messianic powers. Here is the new leader sent by God to the German people in their hour of greatest need.'

Houston Stewart Chamberlain

It is one of the great ironies of world history that the man who had arguably the most profound influence on defining Nazi ideology was an Englishman. Houston Stewart Chamberlain (1855–1927) was the son of an English admiral who had become a naturalized German citizen after marrying the daughter of Richard Wagner with whom he shared an all-consuming passion for the dark side of German romanticism. As with most converts, he became more zealous than those born to the cause leading him to state that 'God builds today upon the Germans alone'. He was, by all accounts, hypersensitive and given to imagining that he was being pursued by the mythical creatures from which his famous father-in-law derived inspiration. Even the level-headed American journalist William L. Shirer, author of the definitive history of the period, *The Rise And Fall of the Third Reich* (1960), took Chamberlain's ravings seriously.

'Chamberlain was given to seeing demons who, by his own account, drove him relentlessly to seek new fields of study. Once in 1896, when he was returning from Italy, the presence of a dream became so forceful that he got off the train at Gardone, shut himself up in a hotel room for eight days and ... wrote feverishly on a biological thesis until he had the germ of the theme that would dominate all his later works: race and history ... Since he felt himself goaded on by demons, his books were written in the grip of a terrible fever, a veritable trance, a state of self-induced intoxication so that ... he was often unable to recognize them as his own work.'

It is a tragedy then that so much of his output was unworthy of a man of his energies and supposed intellect. It was Chamberlain's contention that the white race was superior in every respect, but that it too was degenerate. Only the Teutons were worthy of being called cultured and were to be credited with fashioning the foundations of western civilization. Even the Italian architects of the Renaissance were of Teutonic descent. Needless to say, he blamed the Jews for 'infecting the Indo-Europeans' with impure blood and warned that if inter-marriage continued all non-Jews would eventually become 'a herd of pseudo-Hebraic mestizos, a people beyond all doubt degenerate physically, mentally and morally'.

In 1899, he published his vile theories in what was to become the 'gospel of the Nazi movement'. No one doubted him when he declared that *The Foundations of the Nineteenth Century* had been dictated to him by demons.

It was Chamberlain who first propagated the ridiculous lie that Jesus was a blue-eyed, blond-haired Aryan and that only Germany was worthy of the blessing of a new messiah. In the years prior to the outbreak of the Great War, Chamberlain thought he had identified his saviour in the unlikely form of Kaiser Wilhelm II. He became the Kaiser's confidant and spiritual advisor at the same time as Rasputin was serving a similar role in the Russian palaces of power. But while Rasputin advised restraint, Chamberlain urged the pompous, impetuous German monarch to act in defence of his country's honour. Chamberlain wanted war in order to see his adopted homeland seize its rightful place as master of Europe. He was to be bitterly disappointed.

Then, in 1923, he met Adolf Hitler and declared that the

British political philsopher and racist, Houston Stewart Chamberlain (1855–1927), whose work heavily influenced Nazi ideology.

saviour of the Aryan race was at hand. The following day he wrote to the Nazi leader giving his blessing – and betraying his naivety.

> *'You have mighty things to do, but in spite of your will power I do not take you to be a violent man ... There is a violence that comes out of and leads back to chaos, and there is a violence whose nature it is to form a cosmos. It is in this cosmos building sense that I wish to count you among the up building, not among the violent men ... Nothing*

*can be done as long as the parliamentary system rules: God
knows the Germans have no spark of talent for this system.
Its prevalence I regard with the greatest misfortune for it
can only lead again and again into a morass and bring to
naught all plans for restoring the Fatherland and lifting
it up ... My faith in the Germans has never wavered for
a moment, but my hope I must own, had sunk to a low
ebb. At one stroke you have restored the state of my soul.
That in the hour of her deepest need Germany has given
birth to a Hitler proves her vitality, as do the influences
emanating from him, for these two things, personality and
influence, go together ... May God protect you!'*

Hitler took the old man's words to heart. Within a year he was to
take drastic measures to circumvent the 'parliamentary system'
and be done with democracy for the duration.

FALSE DAWN

'History is made in the street.'

Joseph Goebbels

The story of the abortive Munich Beer Hall Putsch of November
1923 has been documented in detail in numerous accounts of the
rise and fall of Hitler's Reich, most of which agree that it was an
embarrassing debacle for the impatient and ill-organized nascent
Nazi party. Hitler had stormed into the hall with his brown-

shirted SA thugs led by Wilhelm Frick, disrupting a meeting of rival revolutionaries and taking several officials hostage. But he failed to order the seizure of key strategic posts around the city and, after he foolishly allowed his hostages to leave with nothing but their word of honour that they would go home quietly, they naturally raised the alarm.

By the time the Nazis had taken to the streets there was an armed detachment waiting at the main square to greet them with a withering volley of rifle fire. General Ludendorff, the hero of the First World War whom Hitler had persuaded to act as an authoritative figurehead, was allowed to retain his dignity and was offered safe passage through the cordon of bristling bayonets while the would-be revolutionaries scattered in all directions. Goering was seriously wounded, but managed to stagger to a local doctor who refused to treat him. Ironically, it was a Jewish family in an adjacent apartment who gave sanctuary to the former First World War fighter ace and dressed his wound until he could be smuggled into temporary exile in Italy where he numbed the pain and his bruised ego with increasing doses of morphine. It may have been this act of kindness which influenced Goering to later act in defence of certain Jews and declare, 'I will decide who is a Jew and who is not.' Hitler, meanwhile, had scuttled for safety to a waiting car, leaving his leaderless comrades to face the advancing troops. When the smoke had cleared, only Himmler remained. Apparently he cut such an unimposing figure that the troops simply ignored him and he was able to walk to the nearest railway station where he caught the last train home.

Hitler's shock troops take to the streets of Munich in November 1923. Their putsch (coup) failed dismally.

THE TRIAL OF ADOLF HITLER

At his trial, Hitler faced a panel of judges who were clearly in sympathy with his cause, or at least shared his distrust of the anti-monarchist Weimar Republic which they believed was undermining traditional German values. He was allowed to commandeer the dock as his personal forum from where he played to the packed press gallery with all the bluster and bravado of a ham actor.

'The man who is born to be a dictator is not compelled. He wills it. He is not driven forward, but drives himself. The man who feels called upon to govern a people has no right to

say, "If you want me, summon me, I will cooperate." No!
It is his duty to step forward.'

And he concluded his defence with an impassioned plea to providence.

'It is not you, gentlemen, who will pass judgement on us.
  'You may pronounce us as guilty a thousand times over,
but the Goddess of the eternal court of history will smile
and tear to tatters the brief of the state prosecutor and the
sentence of this court. For she acquits us.'

Hitler was sentenced to a nominal five years in the comparative comfort of Landsberg prison with a panoramic view of the River Lech. He was even allowed to retain his deputy, the doggedly devoted Rudolf Hess, to act as his servant and secretary.

LUCIFER'S SERVANT

Hess was a brooding, beetle-browed introvert who, like Hitler, had lived under the shadow of a domineering father. When he saw Hitler speak in 1921, he recognized the qualities that were lacking in himself and was overjoyed to discover that the Führer responded to slavish hero worship. If Hess could be said to possess one quality, it was that of unquestioning obedience. '… One man remains beyond all criticism,' he told a hushed audience at Nuremberg in 1934, 'that is the Führer. This is because everyone feels and knows: he is always right, and he will always be right.'

In 1945, when he stood in the dock at the international war crimes trial held in that same city, his unfailing faith in his Führer remained undiminished.

> *'It was granted me for many years of my life to live and work under the greatest son whom my nation has produced … I regret nothing.'*

But not everyone in the regime found Hess agreeable. He was described by his professor Karl Haushofer (*see below*) as an unsettling presence.

> *'He was one student among others, not particularly gifted, of slow intellectual grasp and dull in his work. He was very dependent on emotions and passionately liked to pursue fantastic ideas. He was only influenced by arguments of no importance at the very limits of human knowledge and superstition; he also believed in the influence of the stars on his personal and political life … I was always disconcerted by the expression of his clear eyes, which had something somnambulistic about it.'*

The 'fantastic ideas' to which Haushofer referred included astrology, clairvoyance and alternative medicine, which were not strange in themselves, but it was Hess's application of the esoteric arts which led many in the party to label him as an eccentric. On one occasion he wrote to every *Gauleiter* (district governor) in the land, requesting a sample of soil from their region so that he could sprinkle it under his baby's cradle as part of an ancient magical 'blessing' rite. Goebbels typically responded in his usual facetious way by offering to post a paving slab from Berlin.

MEIN KAMPF

So long as Hess kept his fringe ideas to himself, Hitler was content to employ him. It was Hess who recorded his leader's muddled stream of racist invective which was to be edited into some semblance of order by Max Amann who published it as *Mein Kampf* ('My Struggle'). The original title – *Viereinhalb Jahre des Kampfes gegen Lüge, Dummheit und Feigheit* ('Four-and-a-half Years of Struggle against Lies, Stupidity and Cowardice') – gives a clear indication of Hitler's agitated mental state at this time and what Gerald Suster, author of *Hitler and the Age of Horus* (1981), called 'the poverty of Hitler's intellect'. It is revealing that the first part of the book is a highly derivative, incoherent rant peppered with blatant falsehoods, while the latter part shows at least a superficial understanding of the principles of geopolitics and the uses to which propaganda can be put. The former betrayed the influence of Eckart, while the latter was down to the influence of a respected academic who was a regular visitor to Hitler's rooms at Landsberg at the invitation of his former pupil, Rudolf Hess.

Professor Karl Haushofer (1869–1945) had served with distinction in the Great War and had risen to the rank of general. It was rumoured that he possessed clairvoyance and had been able to predict the precise time and location of enemy offensives and bombardments which helped to halt several Allied advances. Not surprisingly, perhaps, his military experiences infused his teaching with an aggressive pro-nationalist perspective. He had told Hess and his fellow students:

> '*I intend to teach Political-Geography as a weapon to reawaken Germany to fulfil its destined greatness. I shall re-educate the whole nation to an awareness of the role of geography in history so that every young German shall cease to think parochially but think instead in terms of whole continents.*'

It was Haushofer who conceived the idea of *Lebensraum*, or living space, with which Hitler sought to excuse his insatiable appetite for conquest. And it was Haushofer who can be credited with shaping Hitler's unfocused ramblings into a reasoned argument that brought nationalism out of the beerkellers and into the homes and workplaces of ordinary Germans. Haushofer defended his part in shaping Nazi racist doctrine by arguing

Hitler (front left) in Landsberg Prison after the failed putsch of November 1923. His future deputy, Rudolf Hess, to whom he dictated Mein Kampf, *is standing directly behind him.*

that he was merely one of a number of 'intellectuals' to have influenced Hitler's thinking, but even his own son Albrecht was not fooled by his father's affected innocence. While awaiting execution for his part in the July '44 bomb plot, Albrecht penned a poem which ended with the following lines:

'My father broke the seal –
He sensed not the breath of the Evil One
But set him free to roam the world.'

THE DEVIL'S ADVOCATE

According to Trevor Ravenscroft, the professor's influence was even more insidious than history has acknowledged. 'Haushofer awakened Hitler to the real motives of the Luciferic Principality which possessed him so that he could become the conscious vehicle of its evil intent in the 20th century.' It has become customary for crypto-historians to recast Haushofer as a closet Satanist who had assumed the role of Mephistopheles in order to instruct Hitler in a secret esoteric doctrine derived in part from Madame Blavatsky's Atlantean-based Theosophy and the Wotan-worshipping brotherhoods of the German *völkisch* occultists. But in *Mein Kampf*, Hitler scorns the pseudo-pagan revivalists, such as von List, whose sole 'satanic' ceremony extended to burying empty wine bottles in the shape of a swastika on a mountain top, while swearing an oath of allegiance to the old gods.

> 'I *warn again and again against those wandering* völkisch *scholars whose positive achievement is always nothing, but whose conceit cannot be matched ... The characteristic of most of these natures is that they abound in old German heroism, that they revel in the dim past, stone axes, spears and shields, but that in their own essence they are the greatest imaginable cowards. For the same persons who wave about toy swords, carefully manufactured in imitation of old Germanic style, and wear a prepared bearskin with bull's horns to cover their*

bearded heads, always preach for the present time only a spiritual battle and then run away from the sight of a communist blackjack ... I got to know these people too well not to feel disgust at this miserable comedy. They make a ridiculous impression on the broad masses and the Jew has every reason to spare these völkisch *comedians, to prefer them to the true fighters for the coming Reich. Despite all proofs of their total inability these people pretend to understand everything better than anybody else ... Especially in regard to the so-called religious reformers of the ancient Germanic type, I have the feeling that they are sent by dark forces who do not desire the rebirth of our people. For their entire activity leads the Volk away from its fight against the common enemy, the Jew, in order that it may expend its energy in internal religious struggles.'*

TEA AND SYMPATHY

It is doubtful that Haushofer initiated Hitler into an occult brotherhood as several writers have claimed. The extent of his influence was limited to the degree to which he opened Hitler's eyes to the practical application of geopolitics and the fact that he introduced the dictator in waiting to the concept of *Lebensraum*. It has been assumed that the professor was a secret Satanist simply because Hitler emerged from Landsberg prison in the autumn of 1924 with a renewed appetite for politics and in full command of forces which had previously been unfocused. But this was entirely due to Haushofer's sobering influence in persuading Hitler to channel his energies into effecting change through non-violent means. During his frequent visits, the professor had talked quietly of the need to undermine the foundations of the republic by force of argument rather than force of arms. He explained that, instead of quenching his thirst with beer after a rousing speech and risking becoming belligerent, Hitler would be better off drinking sweet tea and remaining in control. From that moment on, Hitler refused to touch alcohol and became a vegetarian. He also taught Hitler how to present himself as an authoritative figure by dropping his trademark riding crop and adopting instead a statesmanlike posture. And he demonstrated the efficacy of pausing to formulate one's thoughts rather than speaking off the cuff. In effect, Haushofer groomed Hitler for public office. How effective he was in transforming the ragged agitator into an electable leader can be gleaned from the share of the votes the Nazis accrued in subsequent elections until 30 January 1933 when they stormed to power and Hitler found himself a key player on the world stage.

LIFTING A CURSE

Hitler's accession was neither meteoric, nor untroubled. The popularity of his party rose and fell throughout the 1920s in relation to the unemployment figures and the rate of inflation. When the German economy picked up in mid-decade, support for extremists on all sides dwindled and the Nazis lost a significant number of seats in the Reichstag, the German parliament. When the shock waves from the Depression hit Europe in 1929, public resentment against 'Jewish capitalists' and fear of a communist revolution brought indignant, fearful voters out in strength to protest, thus helping the Nazis to consolidate their earlier success. But on the eve of the 1932 election there was every reason to predict another setback for Hitler. President Hindenburg, the staunch elder statesman of pre-war Germany, was losing patience with the extremists and had the power to suspend parliament if he believed that the stability of the republic was under threat. He made no effort to hide his disdain for Hitler whom he considered an undisciplined, rabble-rousing upstart and the Nazis themselves had given him sufficient cause to act. They had brought their beerkeller tactics into the corridors of power where they publicly harangued opposition speakers, staged mass walk-outs and engaged in physical attacks on rival members. But cracks were beginning to appear within their ranks, threatening to divide the party into warring factions and worse – senior German staff officers had confided their fears to Hindenburg concerning the growth of the SA, which had become a vast, unruly private army.

To cap it all, on 30 October, Hitler's mistress Eva Braun attempted suicide for reasons that were never disclosed although Hitler's bizarre and humiliating sexual demands and his stifling jealousy no doubt played a part. Thus it was a distracted, demoralized Nazi leader who entered the political arena the following week and as a result the party lost more seats to their communist rivals. In desperation, Hitler summoned an old friend from his days in Vienna, the astrologer and practitioner of the occult, Erik Jan Hanussen. It was Hanussen (real name Herschel Steinschneider), a Jew, who had taught the Nazi leader how to project his voice and use his hands to emphasize his emotions and keep the audience in his thrall. With his dyed blond hair and aristocratic features, the former carnival performer cut an imposing figure in the Berlin social scene where he cast horoscopes and demonstrated his mastery of his latest obsession, hypnotism. It was in the former capacity that Hitler called Hanussen to his side that bleak winter day.

The portents were bad. Hitler's horoscope revealed that he had been cursed, but by whom and for what reason even Hanussen could not say. The curse may have been commissioned by a political rival, or a spurned and spiteful female admirer. Or it may have been self-inflicted, a suffocating aura of depression brought on by Eva's suicide attempt or his own agitated emotions. Whatever the origin, Hanussen had the answer. It was necessary for someone to travel to Hitler's hometown and there find a mandrake root growing in a butcher's backyard. The mandrake was traditionally a potent aphrodisiac and an amulet of protection. The man-shaped tuber was said to emit a hideous shriek when torn out of the ground and for that reason the witch or magician had to stop their ears with cotton or use a familiar (a cat or dog) to tear it out by the roots. Hitler's reaction to this pronouncement is not recorded, but Hanussen volunteered to journey to Austria and at midnight on a night of the full moon he tore up a mandrake from a suitable site. When he returned to Berlin on New Year's Day 1933, he was able to announce that the curse had been lifted and Hitler's rise to power would resume forthwith. Within 30 days, Adolf Hitler was Chancellor of Germany. On February 27, he became dictator of the new Nazi state after persuading Hindenburg to approve the Enabling Act, granting the Nazis emergency powers. The pretext was the burning of the Reichstag which was blamed on the communists, but was undoubtedly committed by a party impatient for power.

Hanussen had predicted the fire the night before during a séance at his 'Palace of Occultism', but he failed to foresee his own death just six weeks later by unknown hand in a forest outside Berlin.

HITLER CLAIMS THE SPEAR

'A time of brutality approaches of which we ourselves can have absolutely no conception. Indeed, we are already in the middle of it. We shall only reach our goal if we have enough courage to destroy, laughingly to shatter what we once held holy, such as tradition, upbringing, friendship and human love ...'

Joseph Goebbels

On 12 March 1938, as Hitler prepared to enter Vienna to formally announce the annexation of Austria, his acolytes believed their messiah's time had come, but Hitler knew that until he held the Holy Lance in his hands his grip on power could be loosened at any moment. History had taught him that all who seize authority by force had reason to believe that it might be wrested from their grasp, and experience had confirmed his fears. Only four years earlier an assassin had attempted to kill him in the grounds of Goering's estate outside Berlin, but had succeeded only in wounding Himmler. The Reichsführer SS was beside himself with gratitude at having been permitted by providence to shed blood for his Führer and would thereafter remind everyone he met that he was now Hitler's 'blood brother'. The incident had been blamed on disaffected factions within the SA who accused Hitler of having broken his promise to accord them equal pay and rank with the regular army.

Hitler's response to the prospect of a coup was swift and terrible – a four-day-long settling of old scores known as 'The Night of the Long Knives'. It was in anticipation of a similar attempt that Hitler chose to delay his triumphant entry into the capital of the Hapsburg Empire, for although the threat of a counter-revolution was long past, there were rumours that a group of army officers might make a pre-emptive strike to decapitate the dictatorship and so prevent war. So while Hitler awaited his 'loyal Heinrich's' assurance that a security sweep had been completed, he visited his birthplace near Linz and laid flowers on his mother's grave.

When the Führer's motorcade finally made its way into the Imperial capital through the delirious crowds on either side of the Ringstrasse and on to the Heldenplatz, Hitler had the bittersweet satisfaction of returning to the spot where he had stood 30 years earlier as a hungry, penniless artist. The sea of faces parted before him as he strode across the square into the Imperial Palace and on to the balcony from which he would make an historic proclamation accepting his homeland into the greater Reich. But while the crowd surged forward, acclaiming him with cries of *Sieg Heil* and the Nazi salute, the object of their adoration had something more pressing on his mind – the need to take hold of the Spear of Destiny. Ever since that day in the Hofburg in 1913 when Hitler had sensed its inexplicable force coursing though his body, it had lain inert on the faded red velvet cushion behind a glass cabinet awaiting the next leader courageous enough to invoke its power. Now that Hitler was only minutes from possessing it, he must have burned with fever like an addict within sight of his next fix.

In his haste to secure the lance that had been borne through the ages by Europe's greatest conquerors, he brusquely refused an invitation to tour the city and to dine with the civic dignitaries. Even the prospect of lording it over the people who had refused to recognize his existence all those years ago held no appeal for him now. He had one thought and one thought alone – to possess the spear. The wait must have been intolerable, but at least he knew that the precious relic had been secured by a detachment of the SS, personally supervised by Himmler – one of only a handful of men in all Germany beside himself who understood the true value of the spear.

That night, while Austrian Nazis took to the streets in raucous celebration of their success and the citizens of the city of waltzes indulged in a spate of Jew baiting which appalled even their Nazi masters, Hitler and his gang left their suite at the Imperial Hotel en route for the Hofburg. Inside, waiting to greet them were Ernst Kaltenbrunner, Führer of Austria, Major Walter Buch, who was to ensure the legal transfer of the royal regalia to the Reich, and Wolfram von Sievers, head of the Nazi occult bureau.

The entourage waited outside while Hitler and Himmler ascended the staircase to the treasure house where the spear was on display. Minutes later, Himmler returned alone leaving the Führer to fulfil the pledge he had made to himself in that very room 25 years before – to return and claim the Holy Lance for his own diabolical crusade. As Hitler stood before the trophies of the imperialist past he knew that he now held more than history in his hand – he had the whole world within his grasp.

Invoking a century-old precedent for the regalia's removal to Germany, the Holy Lance and the imperial crown jewels were removed from their case, packed in crates and transported in an armoured train under SS guard to Nuremberg where they were put on public view in the crypt of St Catherine's Church – the site of the medieval song contests immortalized in Wagner's *Die Meistersinger von Nürnberg*. The most sacred relic in all Christendom was now in the dark heart of Hitler's evil empire.

THE RECKONING

Allied bombing in the latter years of the war prompted Kaltenbrunner to order the lance and regalia to be removed to the main vault in Kohn's bank on the Königstrasse. But after that building too suffered damage in an air raid, Himmler decided to place the spear out of harm's way. He settled on an ambitious plan to re-open a labyrinth of tunnels several hundred feet under the castle which had been sealed since the Middle Ages. Engineers were brought in and sworn to secrecy before being permitted to work on the project, widening and extending the ancient passageways, digging out a concrete bunker in which they were to install air conditioning before sealing the complex behind a pair of massive steel doors. But as the Allies drew nearer, in March 1945, Himmler ordered the stolen treasures to be smuggled out of the city at night after a decoy convoy had made a show of loading wooden crates and driving them out of town in broad daylight with sirens blaring. The official story circulated among the inquisitive population was that the Hapsburg treasure was to be unceremoniously dumped in Lake Zell near Salzburg.

In fact, the imperial insignia had remained in the city not far from their original resting place, hidden underground in a vault at the Panier Platz. The idea was that they would remain there as a symbol of a rearguard resistance movement codenamed 'Werwolf', which ultimately failed to materialize. Instead, the war-weary *Wehrmacht* capitulated en masse, while the high-ranking officers and war criminals fled to South America on false passports where they and their stolen loot were welcomed with open arms by their brothers in brutality. Only the fanatical SS made a last stand to defend their heartland, 20,000 sacrificing themselves to honour their oath to their Führer, one group repulsing nine assaults by the US 45th Division in a vain attempt to deny the enemy the Nazi Congress Hall, scene of so many grandstanding speeches. When the fighting finally ceased on 20 April, nothing but the rubble-strewn shell of the historic city remained.

Ten days later, a platoon of GIs moving through Obere Schmiedgasse, a street below the castle, chanced to discover the original hiding place of the regalia which had been exposed to the daylight by a recent artillery barrage. They posted a guard in front of the steel doors of the vault and returned to the castle which now served as the headquarters of the American 7th Army to report their find.

It was 2 o'clock in the afternoon. An hour and a half later, the Americans entered the vault and gasped in astonishment at the shoulder-high heaps of Nazi loot which spilled out on to the floor. In the centre was the altar that had been taken for safekeeping from St Catherine's Church and upon it rested a narrow wooden casket. Someone had evidently failed to recognize the significance of the spear and had transferred only the Imperial Crown Jewels to the second site under Panier Platz. The Americans had acquired the Holy Lance.

Several hundred miles away in Berlin, at 3.30 pm, Adolf Hitler relinquished his claim to the spear and shot himself through the mouth. His mistress, Eva Braun, lay lifeless by his side. She had swallowed cyanide. In contrast to their dream of a Wagnerian state funeral, Hitler and his mistress were carried out of the Reichschancellery bunker and cremated in the nearest shell-hole, while Goebbels served as the sole witness. After just 12 years, Hitler's 1,000-year Reich had come to an ignominious end.

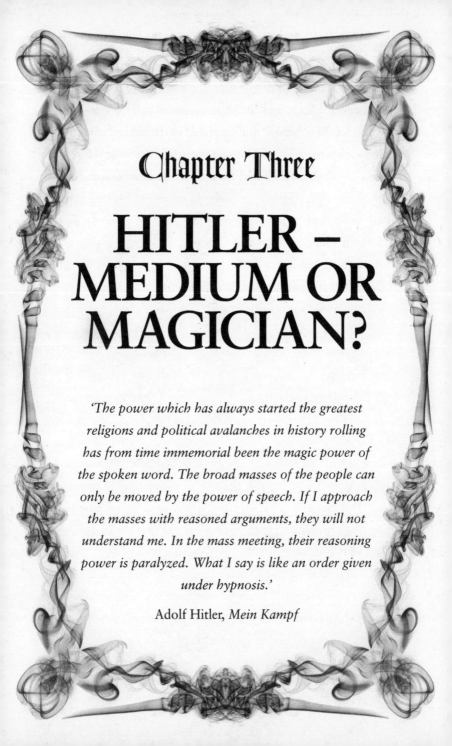

Chapter Three

HITLER – MEDIUM OR MAGICIAN?

'The power which has always started the greatest religions and political avalanches in history rolling has from time immemorial been the magic power of the spoken word. The broad masses of the people can only be moved by the power of speech. If I approach the masses with reasoned arguments, they will not understand me. In the mass meeting, their reasoning power is paralyzed. What I say is like an order given under hypnosis.'

Adolf Hitler, *Mein Kampf*

It is evident from Hitler's own words that he did not acknowledge the existence of evil or the devil, despite having been raised a Catholic, but like so many psychologically flawed individuals he believed that his *Weltanschauung* was unshakable and that he was incapable of being wrong. He was, to use a modern psychological term, the typical 'right man' who will cut off his own nose to spite his face.

Like a Chicago gang leader, Hitler held his unruly mob together, as he did his country, through the twin pillars of totalitarian power – fear and adoration. His simple strategy of divide and conquer ensured that his ministers were too busy jostling for position, defending their own territory and competing for his favours to conspire for his removal. He achieved this by giving the same responsibilities to more than one minister, which generated personal enmity and distrust. Goering disliked Speer, Ribbentrop, Goebbels and Bormann; Goebbels loathed Goering, Ribbentrop and Bormann; Ribbentrop couldn't tolerate anyone and in turn they all despised him. It was the perfect formula for ensuring unquestioning obedience, but it meant that the system was rotten from the inside and fated to fail. The only question was when. Those who had the courage to act did so too late and ineffectively. The failed bomb plot of July 1940 only stiffened the common soldier's resolve to fight on to the bitter end. He assumed that the Führer's life had again been saved by divine intervention.

At Nuremberg in 1946, Albert Speer put the depth of Hitler's hypnotic hold over the German people down to technology.

> 'Hitler's dictatorship differed in one fundamental point from all its predecessors in history. His was the first dictatorship in the present period of technical development, a dictatorship which made complete use of all technical means for the domination of its own country. Through technical means like the radio and the loud-speaker, eighty million people were deprived of independent thought. It was thereby possible to subject them to the will of one man.'

But the French rationalist philosopher, Denis de Rougemont, was prepared to accept a supernatural explanation.

> 'Some people believe, from having experienced in his presence a feeling of horror and an impression of supernatural power, that he is the seat of ... hierarchical spirits which can descend into any ordinary mortal and occupy him ... Where do the superhuman powers he shows on these occasions come from? It is quite obvious that a force of this kind does not belong to the individual and indeed could not even manifest itself unless the individual were of no importance except as the vehicle of a force for which our psychology has no explanation ... What I am saying would be the cheapest form of romantic nonsense were it not that what has been established by this man

or rather – through him – is a reality that is one of the wonders of the century.'

The 'superhuman powers' de Rougemont refers to are not, however, unnatural, nor should they be credited to the influence of a discarnate entity. Hitler's capacity for revitalizing his allies and subordinates has been replicated by true mystics such as George Gurdjieff who developed the ability which Hitler appears to have generated unconsciously.

On one occasion, a male student came to the guru complaining of exhaustion and was revitalized by an infusion of energy consciously directed from mentor to pupil as one would conduct electricity from a charger to a spent battery. The student noted, however, that Gurdjieff was visibly drained by the process and had to retire to recharge himself using meditation.

Historians are now extremely reluctant to use Hermann Rauschning as a reference, but he is useful as a source of anecdotal evidence, the following being a case in point. He wrote:

'A person close to me, told me that [Hitler] wakes up in the night screaming and in convulsions. He calls for help and appears to be half paralysed. He is seized with a panic that makes him tremble until the bed shakes. He utters confused and unintelligible sounds, gasping as if on the point of suffocation. The same person described to me one of these fits with details that I would refuse to believe had I not complete confidence in my informant.

> 'Hitler was standing up in his room, swaying, and looking all around him as if he were lost. "It's he, it's he," he groaned; "he's come for me!" His lips were white, he was sweating profusely. Suddenly he uttered a stream of meaningless figures, then words and scraps of sentences. It was terrifying. He used strange expressions strung together in bizarre disorder. Then he relapsed again into silence, but his lips still continued to move. He was then given a friction and something to drink. Then suddenly he screamed: "There! There! Over in the corner! He is there!" – all the time stamping with his feet and shouting. To quieten him he was assured that nothing extraordinary had happened and finally he gradually calmed down. After that he slept for a long time and became normal again.'

Given the nature of the allegations against Rauschning, we have to assume this is yet another example of Nazi myth-making. Certainly, the allusions to 'unintelligible sounds', 'meaningless figures' and 'scraps of sentences' sound like a poor attempt to convey the 'words of power' by someone who clearly has no idea what a real magician would say or do.

As for the exhortations suggestive of a demonic presence – 'He's over there!' – it is evident that it's yet another pitiable, utterly unconvincing attempt to convey horror. Unfortunately, such transparent attempts to make the nonentities of the Nazi regime more exotic figures only serve to distract from the real source of their power.

POWER OF THE WORD

It was surely no coincidence that Winston Churchill was serving as Britain's Prime Minister at the same time that his nemesis was urging the German people to world domination. Churchill was the antithesis of the ranting Austrian bully. While Hitler spat bile, the well-read and erudite grandson of the 7th Duke of Marlborough expressed the mood of the moment as eloquently as any of England's greatest poets, raising the morale of a nation and stiffening its sinews for the struggle ahead.

In contrast, Hitler wielded the spoken word like a blunt instrument, bludgeoning his enemies into submission. He shared Goebbels' belief that if one told a lie often enough and with conviction the public would eventually accept it as the truth. But how did he manage to defy President Lincoln's famous truism and fool all of his people all of the time?

Many who witnessed his slow-burning speeches at first hand were convinced that he had allowed himself to be possessed by a power greater than himself. Rauschning, who was an astute observer of Hitler's character despite having allegedly fabricated his intimate conversations with the leader, wrote:

'One cannot help thinking of him as a medium. For most of the time, mediums are ordinary, insignificant people. Suddenly, they are endowed with what seems to be supernatural powers, which sets them apart from the rest of humanity. These powers are something that is something outside their true personality ... The medium *is possessed. Once the crisis is passed, they fall back again into mediocrity. It was in this way, beyond any doubt, that Hitler was possessed by forces outside of himself – almost demonical forces of which the individual man, Hitler, was only a temporary vehicle. The mixture of the banal and the supernatural created that insupportable duality of which power was conscious in his presence ... It was like looking at a bizarre face whose expression seemed to reflect an unbalanced state of mind coupled with a disquieting impression of hidden power.'*

This apparent ability to channel another voice, whether from his own subconscious or an external source, was evidently something Hitler had developed from an early age. His childhood friend August Kubizek was struck by the transformation which occurred whenever Adolf was inspired.

'It was as if another being spoke out of his body and moved him as much as it did me. It was not at all a case of a speaker carried away by his own words. On the contrary; I rather felt as though he himself listened with astonishment and emotion to what burst forth from him with elemental force ... like floodwaters breaking their dykes, his words burst from him. He conjured up in grandiose inspiring pictures his own future and that of his people. He was talking of a Mandate which, one day, he would receive from the people to lead them from servitude to the heights of freedom – a

special mission which would one day be entrusted to him.'
[*From* Young Hitler – The Story of our Friendship (1951)]

Gregor Strasser, a comrade from the beerkeller days, was also struck by the physical transformation which overtook Hitler whenever he spoke.

> *'Listen to Hitler and one suddenly has a vision of one who will lead mankind to glory. A light appears in a dark window. A gentleman with a comic moustache turns into an Archangel. Then the Archangel flies away and there is Hitler sitting down, bathed in sweat with glassy eyes.'*

'A light appears in a dark window': the early days in the Brown House in Munich – foreground right is the Nazi parliamentary deputy, Gregor Strasser, murdered during the 'Night of the Long Knives'.

Gregor's younger brother, Otto Strasser, was nearer the mark when he observed:

> 'He touches each private wound on the raw, liberating the mass unconscious, expressing its inner-most aspirations, telling it what it wants to hear.'

Hitler's effect on adoring audiences has been well documented. Nazi activist Kurt Ludecke heard him speak in 1922.

> 'I studied this slight, pale man, his brown hair parted on one side and falling again and again over his sweating brow. Threatening and beseeching, with small pleading hands and flaming steel-blue eyes, he had the look of a fanatic. Presently my critical faculty was swept away – he was holding the masses, and me with them, under a hypnotic spell by the sheer force of his conviction.'

British theologian, Ernestine Amy Buller, witnessed at first hand the effect the Führer had on his followers. In her autobiography, *Darkness Over Germany* (1943), she recalled her impressions of the Nuremberg Rallies.

> 'I was sitting surrounded by thousands of S.A. men and as Hitler spoke I was most interested at the shouts and more often the muttered exclamations of the men around me,

who were mainly workmen or lower-middle-class types.
"He speaks for me, he speaks for me."

"Ach Gott, he knows how I feel." Many of them seemed
lost to the world around them and were probably unaware
of what they were saying. One man in particular struck me
as he leant forward with his head in his hands, and with a
sort of convulsive sob said: "Gott sei Dank, he understands."

'*My attention was attracted by the face of a young man*
who was leading the cries. His arms were outstretched,
and his face white, as he worked himself into a frenzy. And
when the Führer came there was ecstasy in his face such as
I have never seen and should never expect to see outside an
asylum. As I hurried away to go back to the hotel, I heard
uncontrolled sobbing beside me and saw it was a middle-
aged woman in a bath chair: "Now you can take me away,
I will die happily – I have seen the face of the Führer –
Germany will live."'

Hitler's private secretary from 1942 to 1945, Traudl Junge,
acknowledged her Führer's mysterious hold over women.

'*As a man, he didn't look attractive at all. It was more that*
he personified power – that was his fascination. And also
his presence. He had a way of looking at you with those
eyes, which could really set you alight. And somehow he
was a mythical figure for women. He was a saviour, and he

gave off an aura of power, and that impressed women. Like a Messiah, perhaps.'

The mystery of Hitler's mass appeal becomes self-evident when one knows the circumstances of his childhood neurosis which centred on a hatred of his sadistic, overbearing father and his over-identification with his indulgent, masochistic mother.

The American psychoanalyst, Walter Lang, who had been commissioned to write an in-depth analysis of Hitler's nature for the psychological warfare department of the OSS (later the CIA), concluded that Hitler wooed his audience by unconsciously appealing to their feminine nature.

'In regarding his audience as fundamentally feminine in character, his appeal is directed at a repressed part of their personalities. In many of the German people there seems to be a strong feminine-masochistic tendency which is usually covered over by more "virile" characteristics but which finds partial gratification in submissive behaviour, discipline, sacrifice, etc. Nevertheless, it does seem to disturb them and they try to compensate for it by going to the other extreme of courage, pugnaciousness, determination, etc. Most Germans are unaware of this hidden part of their personalities and would deny its existence vehemently if such an insinuation were made. Hitler, however, appeals to it directly and he is in an excellent position to know what goes on in that region because in him this side of

his personality was not only conscious but dominant throughout his earlier life.'

Lang makes another perceptive observation when he points out that Hitler's repressed sexuality had the effect of directing his vital energy and sensuality into his eyes.

'*When a regression of this kind takes place the sexual instinct usually becomes diffuse and many organs which have yielded some sexual stimulation in the past become permanently invested with sexual significance. The eyes, for example, may become a substitute sexual organ and seeing then takes on a sexual significance. This seems to have happened in Hitler's case for a number of informants have commented on his delight in witnessing strip-tease and nude dancing numbers on the stage ... From all of this it is evident that seeing has a special sexual significance for him. This probably accounts for his "hypnotic glance", which has been the subject of comment by so many writers. Some have reported that at their first meeting Hitler fixated them with his eyes as if "to bore through them". It is also interesting that when the other person meets his stare, Hitler turns his eyes to the ceiling and keeps them there during the interview. Then, too, we must not forget that in the moment of crisis* [on hearing of Germany's surrender in 1918] *his hysterical attack manifested itself in blindness.'*

But talk of magic, mediumship and a messianic aura serves only to divert attention away from the true source of Hitler's power – a genuine gift for rabble-rousing oratory which came from deep within. The French writer Robert Bouchez alluded to it, recalling:

'I looked into his eyes – the eyes of a medium in a trance ... Sometimes there seemed to be a sort of ectoplasm; the speaker's body seemed to be inhabited by something ... fluid. Afterwards he shrank again to insignificance, looking small and even vulgar. He looked exhausted, his batteries run down.'

This suggests that the source of Hitler's personal magnetism was his own dynamic life force and was not the result of malevolent possession. He had unconsciously unleashed the vital energy we all possess which the Chinese call *chi*, the Hindus *prana* and the Nazi occultists *vril*. But instead of focusing it and centring it in himself as a practitioner of yoga would do, he unleashed it in a torrent on those he desired to subdue or influence, draining himself in the process. Lacking the knowledge of the adept who understands how to regenerate their inner power cells, the subtle centres which the Hindus call *chakras* ('wheels'), Hitler was used up – a spent force. In the early years he could draw on his audiences and admirers to restore his energy, but after 1942 he made few public appearances and his belief in his own infallibility was challenged by several assassination attempts and the significant strategic losses in Russia which led him to retreat further and further from reality. After the July bomb plot of 1944, his energies turned inwards and he was literally consumed by his own demons – hatred, self-loathing and paranoid hysteria. In effect, natural laws and his own temperament dictated that Hitler was fated to fail.

Albert Speer had often witnessed Hitler's ability to subdue his subordinates by sheer force of will.

'They were all under his spell, blindly obedient and with no will of their own – whatever the medical term for this phenomenon might be. I noticed during my activities as architect, that to be in his presence for any length of time made me tired, exhausted and void.'

Admiral Karl Dönitz was also aware of the Führer's innate capacity for draining people of their vitality and for this reason he distanced himself physically from his leader.

'I purposefully went very seldom to his headquarters for I had the feeling that I would thus best preserve my power of initiative and also because after several days at headquarters I always had the feeling that I had to disengage myself from his powers of suggestion. I am telling you this because in this connection I was doubtless more fortunate than his staff who were constantly exposed to his power and personality.'

But Hitler was equally capable of infusing others with his energy when it served his purpose. He succeeded in reviving a dejected and devitalized Il Duce.

> 'By putting every ounce of nervous energy into the effort I succeeded in pushing Mussolini back on to the rails. In those four days the Duce underwent a complete change. When he got out of the train on his arrival he looked like a broken old man. When he left again he was in high fettle, ready for anything.'

Even after the assassination attempt of 1944 which had left him badly shaken, Hitler's capacity to dominate those around him by sheer force of personality remained undiminished. Karl Boehm Tettelbach, General Staff Officer at the Wolf's Lair HQ, said:

> 'He impressed me and made me tense ... But the flair Hitler had was unusual. He could revive somebody who was almost ready for suicide and make him feel that he could carry the flag and die in battle. Very strange.'

ONE PEOPLE, ONE LEADER, ONE FATE

> 'It is unbelievable, to what extent one must betray a people in order to rule it.'
>
> Adolf Hitler, *Mein Kampf*

We pride ourselves on being individuals, but as the Nazi era demonstrated, anyone can be swept along on a tide of collective emotion if they allow their instincts to overrule their intellect. This primitive need to be part of the tribe or group is difficult to resist as it is linked to our survival instinct and it requires a concerted effort to retain the sense of individuality when a group is acting as one. The phenomenon was not unique to Nazi Germany. It can be seen today in crowd behaviour at sports events and rock concerts, during times of national crisis, in the irrational devotion of religious cults and in the mentality of the mob. When individuals relinquish their free will and submit to the collective will, they behave like a herd of animals or a flock of birds who act as one without any apparent sign or instruction.

Another danger revealed by the Nazi experience is the tendency of a society to project its strengths and failings on to an individual who will assume the role of mother or father of the nation.

In this way a charismatic leader such as Hitler is empowered to act as a focus for his nation's neurosis, or – to express it in magical terms – to act as the medium to channel the psychic energy of his followers. Hitler may not have been a ritual magician in the traditional sense of the word, but that effectively is what he was, as he consciously exploited the nation's prejudice against the Jews, knowing that the Germans would consent to his plan to make a sacrificial offering of the national scapegoat to exorcise a collective anxiety.

THE FREEMASONS

Hitler's paranoid obsession with Freemasonry originated in his mistaken belief that it was primarily a Jewish esoteric society and that it possessed arcane secrets that could undermine the state if its members were allowed to infiltrate the corridors of power.

'All the supposed abominations, the skeletons and death's heads, the coffins and the mysteries, are mere bogeys for children. But there is one dangerous element, and that is the element that I have copied from them. They form a sort of priestly nobility. They have developed an esoteric doctrine not merely formulated, but imparted through the symbols and mysteries in degrees of initiation. The hierarchical organization and the initiation through symbolic rites, that is to say, without bothering the brain but by working on the imagination through magic and symbols of a cult, all this is the dangerous element I have taken over. Don't you see that our party must be of this character ...? An Order, that is what it has to be – an Order, the hierarchical Order of a secular priesthood ... Ourselves or the Freemasons or the Church – there is room for one of the three and no more ... We are the strongest of the three and shall get rid of the other two.'

THE MANIPULATION OF THE MASSES

As history has shown, it is rarely the more passive human qualities which manifest in the group soul. Notable exceptions occurred under the benign influence of Mahatma Ghandi whose passive revolution forced the English out of India and, not so long ago, in the outpouring of national grief which marked the death of Diana, Princess of Wales. Her sudden and unexpected death touched the long-neglected empathetic qualities in the British psyche. Many people were confounded by their own feelings – unacknowledged for so long.

Hitler's opinion on the subject of mass manipulation is revealing, although we have to wonder if he expressed himself in these precise terms since the source of the following quotes is the discredited Rauschning. But Rauschning was known to have paraphrased passages from Hitler's speeches and informal after-dinner discussions or 'table talks', so it seems reasonable to assume that the substance of this extract, taken from *The Voice of Destruction* (1940), is accurate at least.

> 'My enemies have turned up their noses at me. They have asked, full of envy: "Why is this man so successful with the masses?" ... Was this just a lucky fluke, was it due to the uncritical mind of the masses? No, it was thanks to us, to our assiduity, and to the technique we perfected.

'It is true that the masses are uncritical, but not in the way these idiots of Marxists and reactionaries imagine. The masses have their critical faculties, too, but they function differently from those of the private individual. The masses are like an animal that obeys its instincts. They do not reach conclusions by reasoning. My success in initiating the greatest people's movement of all time is due to my never having done anything in violation of the vital laws and the feelings of the mass. These feelings may be primitive, but they have the resistance and indestructibility of natural qualities. A once intensely felt experience in the life of the masses, like ration cards and inflation, will never again be driven out of their blood. The masses have a simple system of thinking and feeling, and anything that cannot be fitted into it disturbs them. It is only because I take their vital laws into consideration that I can rule them.

'I have been reproached for making the masses fanatic and ecstatic ... I can lead the masses only if I tear them out of their apathy. Only the fanatic mass can be swayed. A mass that is apathetic and dull is the greatest threat to unity.'

Rauschning also noted:

'He had made the masses fanatic, he explained, in order to fashion them into the instruments of his policy. He had awakened the masses. He had lifted them out of themselves, *and given them meaning and a function. He had been reproached with appealing to their lowest instincts. Actually, he was doing something quite different. If he were to go to the masses with reasonable deliberations, they would not understand him. But if he awakened corresponding feelings in them, they followed the simple slogans he presented to them.'*

The Nazi leadership at the Nuremberg Rally, 1936, the highlight of the year for the Party faithful.

Hitler again:

> '*At a mass meeting thought is eliminated. And because this is the state of mind I require, because it secures to me the best sounding-board for my speeches, I order everyone to attend the meetings, where they become part of the mass whether they like it or not, "intellectuals" and bourgeois as well as workers. I mingle the people. I speak to them only as the mass ...*
>
> '*I am conscious that I have no equal in the art of swaying the masses, not even Goebbels. Everything that can be learned with the intelligence, everything that can be achieved by the aid of clever ideas, Goebbels can do, but real leadership of the masses cannot be learned. And remember this: the bigger the crowd, the more easily it is swayed. Also, the more you mingle the classes – peasants, workers, black-coated workers – the more surely will you achieve the typical mass character.*
>
> '*Don't waste time over "intellectual" meetings and groups drawn together by mutual interests. Anything you may achieve with such folk today by means of reasonable explanation may be erased tomorrow by an opposite explanation. But what you tell the people in the mass, in a receptive state of fanatic devotion, will remain like words received under a hypnotic influence, ineradicable, and impervious to every reasonable explanation. But just as the individual has neuroses which*

must not be disturbed, so the mass has its complexes that must not be awakened ... The entire weight of the masses rests on the party, and the party is itself a constituent part of the mass ... Mastery always means the transmission of a stronger will to a weaker one. How shall I press my will upon my opponent? By first splitting and paralysing his will, putting him at loggerheads with himself, throwing him into confusion.

'It's good fortune for the government that the masses don't think, otherwise human society as we know it might cease to exist.'

Chapter Four

ASTROLOGY IN THE THIRD REICH

'Nobody believes in astrology more than Herr Hitler. The best clients of the International Institute in London are the private astrologers in Berchtesgaden. Every month they ask for new astrological documents. This is because Herr Hitler believes in astrology. And he proves it. It is not by accident that his coups are all made in the month of March. Before striking he chooses the most favourable time indicated by the stars. And March is assuredly his best month ...'

Gazette de Lausanne, 5 April 1939

In the spring of 1923, Germany's foremost amateur astrologer, Frau Elsbeth Ebertin, received a letter from an admirer in Bavaria asking her to draw up the horoscope of a man who had just taken control of a minor political party in Munich. The writer had convinced herself that the new leader of the German Workers' Party was destined for great things and she wanted the rest of the nation, which was still recovering from the Great War, to share her hopes for the future. She supplied Frau Ebertin with the date and place of the man's birth as 20 April, 1889 at Braunau am Inn, Austria, but withheld his name.

Accepting the challenge, the seer of Gorlitz, as she was known, duly drew up the chart which she published with a commentary in the 1924 edition of her popular almanac, *Ein Blick in die Zukunft* (A Glimpse into the Future).

Although Frau Ebertin had not been given her subject's time of birth (an essential detail for the casting of an astrological chart), she made an eerily accurate forecast by assuming he was born in the morning and producing what is known as a 'progressed horoscope', which goes beyond a psychological profile to predict the subject's prospects for a specific period in their life. Her chart suggested that this radical political activist did not need to ally himself with dark forces, but merely had to seize the predetermined opportunities that would present themselves in due course to ensure that the prediction would be fulfilled.

She concluded:

'A man of action born on April 20 1889 with the Sun in the twenty-eighth degree of Aries at the time of his birth, can expose himself to personal danger by reckless action and could very likely trigger an uncomfortable crisis. His constellations show that this man is to be taken very seriously indeed; he is destined to play a Führer-role in future battles. The man I have in mind with his strong Aries influence is fated to sacrifice himself for the German nation and to face up to all circumstances with audacity and courage, even when it is a matter of life and death, and to give an impulse which will burst forth quite suddenly to a German freedom movement. But I will not anticipate destiny – time will show but the present state of affairs at the time I write this cannot last.'

The subject of the prediction was, of course, Adolf Hitler, who fulfilled the first part of the prophecy by staging a putsch in the Bavarian capital not long after the publication of Ebertin's almanac. Although the armed uprising was an ignominious failure, Hitler found a sympathetic ear among the judges in court and was able to hijack the proceedings for propaganda purposes.

Frau Ebertin was later rewarded by being granted a private audience with the Nazi leader whom she described as shy and self-conscious in contrast to his public speaking persona when she witnessed the performance of 'a man possessed'.

She subsequently drew up a second, more detailed horoscope based on the assumption that Hitler had been born at 6.22 pm which she considered more likely as this fitted his personality. She concluded her second report with the prophetic words. 'It will turn out that recent events [*meaning the failed putsch*] will not only give this movement inner strength, but external strength as well, so that it will give a mighty impetus to the pendulum of world history.'

HITLER'S HOROSCOPE

The new natal chart revealed that Hitler's birth occurred on the cusp of Aries and Taurus which signified that he could be driven by unchecked ambition. His ascendant (the degree of the Zodiac immediately on the eastern horizon at the moment of birth) was the twenty-fifth degree of Libra and his natal sun was in the first degree of Taurus. This would indicate someone for whom self-expression is an all-consuming passion either through the arts, acting or public speaking. Neptune provides the ability to inspire but can also end in the haranguing of bystanders to no avail. Although Frau Ebertin did not say so, this profile would be likely to produce an evangelical politician or cult leader, and someone who was self-sufficient. But there were other influences which augured ill for this individual, namely a Venus-Mars conjunction which suggested a tendency to stifle a craving for recognition out of fear of rejection. Venus and Mars were also in Taurus, with Mercury in Aries, which emphasized a stubborn, self-centred aspect of his personality which would ensure that

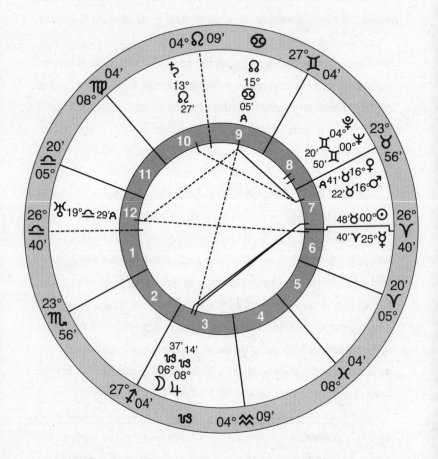

The horoscope of Adolf Hitler: born 6.22 pm, 20 April 1889 at Braunau am Inn, Austria. Astrologers agree that this is the horoscope of a man gifted at public expression, yet one who will find it difficult to listen to the ideas of others.

he would not be easily deterred by delays or obstructions. Nor would he be discouraged by the opinion of other people or swayed by their objections.

The other influential aspect in the chart was Capricorn, another earth sign. In Hitler's chart, both the Moon and Jupiter were in this sign which meant that this pragmatic, hard-headed aspect of his personality was reinforced. But the flip side of this quality is intolerance, for under certain conditions the virtues ordained by the stars can easily become vices. Serious astrologers agree that the stars set out a blueprint for our lives, but free will, not fate, determines each person's destiny and also that of nations.

Of the remaining planets Saturn was in the thirteenth degree of Leo (a fire sign), Uranus was in the twentieth degree of Libra, while Neptune and Pluto were in Gemini (both air signs), thus giving rise to a conflict of emotion and intellect which could lead to spontaneous, ill-considered actions or, conversely, prevarication arising out of fear of being held responsible for the consequences of one's actions.

Although the Sun sign is the most significant factor in determining the main themes in a person's life, it is a popular fallacy that one's future is determined by this aspect alone.

It is, in effect, mediated by what are known as the quadruplicities or qualities – the cardinal (creation), fixed (preservation) and mutable (adjustment) signs. The strength of Taurus, Capricorn and Libra in Hitler's horoscope meant there was an uncommonly strong tendency towards dominance and aggression if his actions were called into question or his plans were frustrated. A creature of habit, he would find it almost impossible to accept change or even consider that another person might have the solution he sought.

Such personalities, when opposed, inevitably undermine their own efforts and ultimately have a tendency to pull down everything around them because they cannot admit even to themselves that they might be wrong.

Another factor in determining the future prospects and actions of an individual are the relative aspects between the planets at the time of their birth. In Hitler's chart, Saturn was square (at 90°) to Mars which indicates a distrustful, suspicious nature. Saturn was also square to Venus in his natal chart which suggests an emotionally confused personality who avoids intimate relationships and may express his sexual nature in unnatural ways. This aspect reveals a self-indulgent idealist who can take duty to an extreme. Such individuals may imagine that they have been born to bear a burden or are destined to suffer because they are misunderstood – a common complaint of the false messiahs who seek followers and lead fanatical religious cults into self-destruction. Mercury in opposition to Uranus compounds the problem by ensuring that the individual is totally self-absorbed, lacking true compassion and preferring to channel his affection into those who will not spurn them such as animals and children.

Saturn sextile (at 60°) to Uranus nurtures an authoritarian personality, while Neptune in conjunction with Pluto can incline a weak individual to retreat into self-delusion. Venus in conjunction with Mars emphasizes robust self-confidence, but also a certain inflexibility. People with this aspect see everything in stark black and white and tend to harbour resentments for years, long after the event which gave rise to such feelings.

The Sun trine (at 120°) to the Moon and Jupiter, which were in conjunction, appeared to prefigure success but indicated that this particular subject hungers for status and public approval. In fact, the need for approval and acceptance will be addictive, particularly from those he perceives as having superior social standing, and if it is withdrawn love of the people could turn to hatred as their capriciousness would be viewed as a betrayal of trust. The Moon–Jupiter conjunction often creates immature and flawed personalities who crave attention and can exhibit child-like temper tantrums if deprived of the appreciation they believe they deserve.

In conclusion, the chart reveals an emotionally conflicted, unstable, neurotic and manipulative, self-centred personality whose overriding need to overcome feelings of failure emerges to overcome a lack of self-worth. This would be the assessment of a modern astrologer with a basic understanding of psychology, but, needless to say, Frau Ebertin was highly selective in her reading of the Führer's chart. Other contemporary German astrologers who drew up Hitler's chart were disturbed by what they saw and some even tried to convey their forebodings to those who might do something before it was too late.

With the chart drawn and the numerous planetary influences recognized, it would be possible for an accomplished astrologer to draw up a second chart for a specific date in the future when alignments like those at the moment of birth could be expected again.

Such a date would be seen as exceptionally favourable for taking crucial decisions and, if acted upon, would almost certainly guarantee success. In Hitler's case, such a positioning is believed to have occurred again early in 1940, 10 May being the date he launched his invasion of France, Belgium and Holland. Military historians tend to dismiss the entire astrological aspect out of hand, citing Hitler's desire to give his troops as long a period of dry weather as possible since he was haunted by the prospect of his army becoming bogged down in the muddy fields of Flanders as the German army had been during his own service in the First World War. In the event, his victory in 1940 was so swift and overwhelming that it gave birth to a new strategic term, blitzkrieg (lightning war), and it convinced many in Germany and abroad, who were familiar with the influence the stars can exert on our destiny, that Hitler had been advised by an astrologer.

Frau Ebertin's fate adds a curious postscript to her predictions. She was killed in an Allied air raid in 1944, having refused to leave her home because the townspeople believed that as long as she remained no harm could come to them. According to her son, she had foretold the date of her own death and she also knew which of her neighbours would die on that day because at one time or another she had cast their charts leading her to conclude that they would all die together.

THE CASE FOR ASTROLOGY

Those who do not believe that planetary alignments can influence our lives will argue that Hitler was the product of his upbringing – specifically, a domineering father and an over-indulgent mother – rather than the subtle stresses of cosmic tides. But serious astrologers who operate within a spiritual tradition see more than the external effects noted by the fortune-tellers who draw up horoscopes for the popular press. They will be acutely aware of the invisible mechanism behind the universe which determines the psychological configuration peculiar to each person who is literally a child of their time. Hitler was fated to assume the role he did only in the sense that he gravitated to the centre of the political storm brewing up in Germany at that time because of his psychological make-up. He responded to the nation's call for a leader with his temperament, but if he had not stepped forward a similar individual might have fulfilled the role intended for him. In short, the random factors of Hitler's birth ensured that he was in the right place at the right time to offer Germany the leader it desired and, one might say, deserved.

NOSTRADAMUS AND THE NAZIS

According to many experts in the ancient art of divination, Frau Ebertin was not the first astrologer to foresee the rise of Hitler and his Nazi party. Nostradamus, the 16th-century 'Seer of Salon', is said to have encoded his predictions in a collection of cryptic verses known as the *Centuries* which have been the subject of heated debate for the past 400 years.

It is thought that this 'prince of prophets' obscured the true meaning of his visions because he feared being accused of practising sorcery, but he may also have left them open to interpretation because he intended his verses to be pondered upon by scholars and not by a largely illiterate population who would fear they had no influence over their own lives if the verses proved the existence of predestination. He made this clear in a warning to those seeking to know the future without having first acquired knowledge of the secret art of divination.

'Let those who read this verse ponder its meaning
Let the common crowd and the unlearned leave it alone
All of them – Idiot Astrologers and Barbarians – keep off
He who does the other thing let him be a priest of the rite.'

It is tempting in retrospect to interpret various quatrains as foretelling the rise of Hitler and the outbreak of the Second World War.

'In the farthest depths of Western Europe
A child will be born of a poor family
Who by his speeches will seduce great numbers
His reputation will grow even greater in the eastern domain.'

Perhaps the most celebrated seer of all, the Frenchman Nostradamus: some people credit him with foretelling, among many other things, the rise of Hitler and the Nazi Party in Germany.

Both Hitler's annexation of Austria in 1938 and his adoption of the swastika also appear to have been foreseen.

> *'The great priest of the party of Mars*
> *Who will subjugate the Danube*
> *The cross harried by the crook.'*

And his initial military successes are accurately foretold.

> *'He will transform into Greater Germany*
> *Brabant, Flanders, Ghent, Bruges and Boulogne.'*

Then there is the much-quoted verse:

> *'Hunger-maddened beasts will make the streams tremble*
> *Most of the land will be under Hister*
> *In a cage of iron the great one will be dragged*
> *When the child of Germany observes nothing.'*

This could read as an image of the blitzkrieg of 1940, when German tanks swept across the Franco-Belgian border to occupy the Low Countries. Hitler was regarded at the time as a man who repeatedly failed to honour agreements and treaties making him 'the child of Germany who observes nothing', although the reference to the great one in the 'cage of iron' remains obscure. 'Hister', however, is more likely to refer to the Ister, a classical name for the Danube, making the prediction, 'most of the land will be under Hister', a reference to a flood rather than military invasion.

For those who doubt the possibility that man can foresee the future, it is worth recalling the tale often told of Nostradamus' final prediction. Shortly before his death in 1566, he asked an engraver to inscribe a date on a metal plate to be placed in his coffin alongside his remains. That date was 1700 – the year he predicted he would finally be laid to rest. The engraver did not understand how the seer could be interred 134 years after being buried, but did as he had been asked. Exactly 134 years later, the coffin was exhumed by the French authorities who needed to satisfy themselves that this was indeed the coffin of Nostradamus. So they opened the casket to identify the skeleton and there, clutched in the bony fingers, was the metal plate engraved with the year of his exhumation – 1700.

PROPHECY AND PROPAGANDA

'The enemy is now making use of horoscopes in the form of handbills dropped from planes, in which a terrible future is prophesied for the German people. But we know something about this ourselves! I am having counter-horoscopes worked up which we are going to distribute, especially in the occupied areas.'

Goebbels' Diary, 16 March 1942

During the first months of the Second World War prior to the invasion of France, the Nazis waged a crude but evidently effective psychological campaign against the civilian population of the Low Countries who were then living under the threat of imminent attack. Leaflets were dropped containing pro-Nazi interpretations of the prophecies made by Nostradamus as well as fake astrological magazines in Dutch, French and Flemish containing phoney predictions of future German victories.

Historians attribute the crushing defeat of France, Belgium and Holland in the offensive of May 1940 to purely practical factors – the ingrained defeatism of the French, the superiority of the German forces, their speed and the element of surprise gained by their audacious strategy of attacking through the Ardennes to circumvent the impregnable French defences known as the Maginot Line. But there are those who believe it was the Nazis' employment of psychological warfare which proved highly effective in softening up the opposition and convincing the defenders that resistance was futile. The strategy was considered so successful that it was copied by the Allies later that same year.

The idea had originated with Magda Goebbels, wife of Joseph Goebbels, the Minister of Propaganda and Enlightenment, who had chanced upon a book entitled *Mysteries of the Sun and the Soul* in which the author made a compelling case for interpreting one of the 400-year-old quatrains as foreseeing an expansion of the German Reich after a bloody conflict with France, Britain and Poland. Most astonishing was the naming of the year in which this conflict would take place – 1939 – which had been arrived at by calculating the date from which England would see the monarchy change seven times in a period of 290 years. According to the author, Dr Kritzinger, this could only refer to the period following the execution of Charles I on 30 January 1649. Consequently, Dr Kritzinger was summoned to Goebbels' office on 4 December 1939, where he was invited to identify other verses which might be adopted in support of Nazi policy. Kritzinger was dismayed at the prospect of being recruited by a regime he despised, and so he stalled by playing the absent-minded academic, finally provoking the ever-impatient Goebbels into terminating the interview.

Frustrated, but not discouraged, the Reichsminister, known to his enemies as 'the poison dwarf' on account of his diminished stature and vitriolic tongue, turned for help to a paranoid anti-Semite whom he knew he could count on to compromise his principles in the interests of National Socialism.

KRAFFT

Karl Ernst Krafft (1900–45) was a Swiss-born astrologer whose talents had come to light on 2 November 1939, when he wrote a report for his Gestapo paymaster, Dr Fesel, informing him of an attempt on the Führer's life which would take place in the coming week. Prior to this he had been gainfully employed in drawing up the astrological charts of Winston Churchill and the leaders of the countries Germany expected to be at war with in the coming months in an attempt to forecast their reaction and expose their weaknesses.

Fesel dismissed the warning as the raving of a crank, but was forced to re-examine it when the failed assassination took place as predicted on 8 November. A time bomb placed in a pillar at a Munich beer hall exploded just minutes after the Nazi leader had left the building. Seven party members who had been commemorating the Beer Hall Putsch of 1923 were killed and many others were seriously injured. It has been suggested that the Nazis planted the bomb to be able to accuse their neighbours of attempting a coup, thus giving Hitler an excuse for invasion. Certainly they would have had no second thoughts about sacrificing several of their own if it brought about the desired result, but time bombs were unreliable, making it highly unlikely that the leadership would have risked the device exploding prematurely.

The SS leadership suspected disloyal elements within the Party but were unable to unearth any physical evidence. It is said that in desperation Himmler consulted an Austrian psychic who went into a trance on Himmler's sofa and described three foreigners conspiring with Otto Strasser who was known to have Soviet sympathies.

INNER VOICES

Hitler's narrow escape has been cited as yet another example of the many occasions on which the Führer was saved from certain death by the dark forces he had pledged himself to serve, while conventional historians put the incident down to pure luck. However, there is another, more plausible explanation for Hitler's extraordinary run of good fortune in the early years of his leadership, as well as the precognitive dream he had in the trenches.

In those years, like Joan of Arc, he heeded the inner voice which he had credited with awakening him to his destiny in

Pasewalk military hospital, near Berlin, in 1918 when he was suffering from the effects of mustard gas.

He allowed this inner voice to guide him to the early victories from 1939 to 1941, while his general staff urged caution. Again, orthodox historians would simply attribute Hitler's initial victories to his uncanny ability to read the political situation and anticipate his opponents' reactions.

As for the 'revelation' he experienced in Pasewalk, it seems likely that his alleged blindness was psychosomatic and not due to the gas. His hysterical nature simply could not accept Germany's defeat so he literally refused to 'see' the truth.

'On the 13th October, 1918, I was caught in a heavy British gas attack at Ypres. I stumbled back with burning eyes taking with me my last report of war. A few hours later, my eyes had turned into glowing coals and it had grown dark around me.'

It was while in hospital recovering from his ordeal that he learned of Germany's surrender.

'Everything went black before my eyes; I tottered and groped my way back to the ward, threw myself on my bunk, and dug my burning head into my blanket and pillow. So it had all been in vain. In vain all the sacrifices and privations; in vain the hours in which, with mortal fear clutching at our hearts, we nevertheless did our duty; in

vain the death of two million who died. Had they died for this? Did all this happen only so that a gang of wretched criminals could lay hands on the Fatherland.

'I knew that all was lost. Only fools, liars and criminals could hope for mercy from the enemy. In these nights hatred grew in me, hatred for those responsible for this deed. Miserable and degenerate criminals! The more I tried to achieve clarity on the monstrous events in this hour, the more the shame of indignation and disgrace burned my brow.'

Adolf Hitler, *Mein Kampf*

Dr Heinrich Fesel refused to inform Hitler of Krafft's prediction, fearing he might share the fate of the assassin Georg Elser for having failed to warn the Führer. But Krafft was not prepared to be overlooked. He sent a telegram to Rudolf Hess bragging about his prediction and offering his services and his unswerving loyalty to the Reich.

While Krafft dreamt of fawning at the Führer's feet with his charts under his arm and the fate of nations in his hands, members of the Gestapo were already en route to his front door. They arrested him on suspicion of being a co-conspirator in the November bomb plot, but after many uncomfortable hours of questioning he was able to persuade them that he had merely foreseen the incident in Hitler's horoscope. Goebbels was sceptical of precognition on principle, but was suitably impressed with Krafft's knowledge of his subject. He enlisted the astrologer in his campaign of disinformation and defeatism which culminated with the publication in 1941 of *How Nostradamus Foresaw the Future of Europe*, which put a pro-Nazi spin on the *Centuries*.

Krafft has subsequently been elevated to the role of Hitler's astrologer by historians who assumed his influence was far greater than it was in reality, having been misled by exaggerated claims in Louis de Wohl's sensationalistic autobiography *The Stars in War and Peace* (1952) as well as ill-informed articles in various occult publications.

In fact, Krafft appears to have been little more than a freelance consultant who fell out of favour after 1941 when he failed to repeat his earlier success. Having outlived his usefulness, Krafft was deported to Buchenwald concentration camp in 1942, where he died in 1945, shortly before the end of the war.

THE EMPIRE STRIKES BACK

'In the United States astrologers are at work to prophesy an early end for the Führer. We know that type of work as we have often done it ourselves. We shall take up our astrological propaganda again as soon as possible. I expect quite a little of it, especially in the United States and England.'

Goebbels' Diary, 28 April 1942

In 1940, the war was going badly for the British who were besieged on their beleaguered island from the air by Goering's

Luftwaffe, while their supplies were being sunk by the U-boat 'wolf packs' prowling the treacherous waters of the Atlantic. The bulk of the British Army was still recovering after their miraculous evacuation from Dunkirk, although there was some good news from the 'Second Front' in Africa where the British were discovering that the Italians lacked the fighting spirit of their German allies. Desperate to turn the tide, the British took a leaf out of Goebbels' book and established a covert 'black ops' group to wage their own propaganda war. They enlisted the help of Hungarian émigré and astrologer Luis de Wohl (Ludwig von Wohl-Musciny, 1903–61), a colourful and controversial figure. He was granted the rank of captain after he had convinced them that he could anticipate the advice Hitler would be given by his personal astrologer Karl Krafft, with whom he claimed to have clashed prior to his escape from Germany. An unrepentant fantasist, de Wohl had invented an exotic past for himself which involved a dramatic meeting with Dr Goebbels who, he claimed, had offered him a position in the Propaganda Ministry as resident astrologer – an offer which put de Wohl in conflict with the conspiracy-obsessed Krafft.

On his arrival in England, de Wohl was put to work writing fake predictions for counterfeit copies of a popular German astrological magazine, *Der Zenit*, which were printed in England and smuggled into Germany and the occupied countries. The plan was to convince the Germans that the magazine's prophet was uncommonly accurate by the simple expedient of printing the 'predictions' several months after the events had occurred. The hope was that those who were fooled into believing that the magazine was genuine would then be demoralized by other fictitious forecasts of crushing defeats for the Axis Powers predicted for the coming months. Unfortunately, several crates of the fake publication were intercepted by the Gestapo who noted that the credited editor of the latest issue, Dr Korsch, had been dead for several years.

De Wohl was then shipped off to America in early 1941 where he toured US news networks offering a damning psychological profile of the Nazi leader, which culminated in a prediction of Hitler's imminent death, in the hope that this 'news' would filter back to Berlin.

In retrospect, de Wohl's reading of Hitler's horoscope was surprisingly perceptive. Comparing Hitler's chart with that of Napoleon, de Wohl concluded that they shared the same alignment of Saturn, suggesting that Hitler would die or be overthrown within a few years. He also predicted the violent death of Hitler's mistress, although at the time, no one knew of her existence outside the Nazi inner circle. And he also foresaw defeat for the German Army on the Eastern Front, despite the fact that the Russian campaign had just begun and seemed to presage another lightning victory for the *Wehrmacht*.

The British clearly valued his contributions to the campaign and in 1943, under the auspices of black propaganda spymaster Sefton Delmer, de Wohl spent months in seclusion compiling a 124-page book entitled *Nostradamus prophezeit den Kriegsverlauf* ('Nostradamus Predicts the Course of the War'), which included 50 verses written by himself but attributed to the Seer of Salon and annotated with a scholarly commentary predicting defeat for the Reich.

'THE LOUIS DE WOHL I KNEW'

De Wohl's reputation as a formidable occultist and his own recollection of the part he played in Britain's 'psychic warfare' against the Nazis are as fanciful as one of the popular novels with which he made his name after hostilities ended. It is clear that he revelled in a myth of his own making. For a more objective view, it is worth reading the recollections of his friend and fellow astrologer, Dr Felix Jay, whose evaluation of de Wohl originally appeared in *Traditional Astrologer* magazine (1998) shortly before de Wohl's death. Dr Jay recalled a meeting at de Wohl's apartment in Park Lane, London, in the 1950s, during which the would-be adventurer explained the extent of his role in the British 'black ops'.

'He explained to me that because of his intimate knowledge of the work of Hitler's astrologers and their methods, the British authorities had entrusted him to read their minds and discover what advice they would give the Fuehrer, who, he said, was totally dominated by fortune-tellers. He mentioned one astrologer in particular, Karl Ernst Krafft, whom I had never heard of at that time. The impression he conveyed to me was that he [Krafft] was hob-nobbing with

the General Staff. Further questioning was avoided, quite properly, by reference to the Official Secrets Act. There always had been unsubstantiated rumours of Hitler's pre-occupation with occultism. One such story concerned a Berlin clairvoyant named Hannussen, already fashionable years before Hitler's advent to power, who in 1933 or 1934 mysteriously disappeared. De Wohl has been accused of fabricating a myth: the fact is that he did not create it, but, as he did in many other respects, he probably recognised its material possibilities and he exploited them to the full ... Aware of the general attitude towards astrology, I found it increasingly difficult to believe that the British High Command would consult an enemy-alien astrologer. I came to the conclusion that his work lay in a different direction. Astrologically seen too, there appeared to be a flaw in De Wohl's argument, in that the methods of astrology are not as determined as those of the physical sciences: assuming Hitler did consult astrologers, did Louis know what methods they applied? Personal horoscopes of the principal military and naval chiefs engaged in the struggle were susceptible to something like a common interpretation, but what about mundane maps [astrological charts of nations]?

' ... *in 1952 appeared his last book with an astrological content,* The Stars of War and Peace, *in which he painted a sensational picture of his astrological contribution to the British victory. This book was the culmination of a*

Louis de Wohl (1903–61), author and astrologer, who claimed to have made a significant contribution to the British war effort.

concerted effort on his part to turn whatever his secret work during the war had been into a legend; an effort that, I heard much later, had started with a large number of syndicated articles all over the world. This legend, which proved very lucrative, has since been recognised for what it is, a carefully cultivated myth and not history ...

'Then there is the embarrassing fact of the use of astrology for propaganda purposes during World War II, the exploitation of the bogy of Hitler's belief in the stars, the creation of the image of the 'evil' Krafft – all matters known to me only years afterwards. Whether the prostitution of a science or a belief, the use of phoney predictions, the adulteration of ancient material, like Nostradamus' Centuries is justifiable in war, is an ethical question which the practitioner must answer for himself. It lastly may depend on whether one believes in astrology or not. Did Louis de Wohl believe in astrology? Did he regard it as an esoteric or scientific discipline? I must confess that after the end of the War, I began to doubt it.'

A WARNING TO THE CURIOUS

When attempting to interpret the obscure symbolism of the *Centuries*, it is worth bearing in mind that the Fifth Law of Prophecy – The Law of Diminishing Accuracy – as defined by author Peter Lemesurier. *The Armageddon Script* (1981) states that the accuracy of a prediction will diminish with time. In short, a genuine prophet who limits himself to predicting events in their own time is more likely to have their predictions fulfilled than a seer who peers into the distant future because they will not be able to understand what they are seeing.

It is also a mistake to accept the visions of a symbolist such as Nostradamus at face value as these are open to a number of equally plausible interpretations. Lemesurier contends that if anyone other than a mystic of comparable intuitive ability attempts to interpret such imagery they will encounter the Second Law of Prophecy, that of Thwarted Expectation, which states that a person of lesser vision will come to the obvious conclusions and that these will inevitably be wrong.

And finally, anyone attempting to interpret predictions made by another individual or who desires to draw conclusions from an astrological chart needs to be aware of the Third Law, that of Prejudicial Interference, which makes it clear that predictions and preconceptions do not mix.

FLIGHT OF FANCY

Hitler's attitude towards astrology evidently hardened after Rudolf Hess's misguided peace mission to Scotland in May 1941, which saw the deputy leader of the Nazi Party ignominiously incarcerated in a British prison like a common POW. As SS Brigadeführer Walter Schellenberg observed in his memoirs, 'the great interest that Hitler had previously shown in astrology changed to uncompromising apathy' following Hess's flight.

Deluded Hess may have been suffering from an undiagnosed mental disorder as there can be no other reason why he would get it into his head that he had been charged with a divine mission to bring peace between Britain and Germany at the very moment when the former was bracing itself for a fight for its very survival.

Hitler's initial reaction at the news was to rage that his heir apparent 'had gone crazy', but when he had calmed down, he attributed the embarrassing episode to the advice given to Hess by astrologers who were suspected of being opposed to the Nazi regime. The official explanation for Hess's irrational behaviour was leaked to a Swiss correspondent of *The Times* which published an item in the issue dated 14 May.

> *'Certain of Hess's closest friends have thrown an interesting light upon the affair. They say that Hess has always been Hitler's astrologer in secret. Up to last March he had always predicted good fortune and had always been right. Since then, notwithstanding the victories Germany has won, he has declared that the stars showed that Hitler's meteoric career was approaching its climax.'*

Hess was not, as the report stated, Hitler's astrologer, but he is known to have surrounded himself with those on the fringes of occultism, the aspirants rather than the true adepts. But did the idea for the ill-fated mission originate with a former mentor, Professor Karl Haushofer, who was said to have had a vision of his pupil 'striding through the tapestried halls of English castles, bringing peace between the two great Nordic nations'? Karl's son, Albrecht, was a self-proclaimed adept of 'astral science', an astrologer with a reputation for accuracy and a firm believer that the rise of Hitler had been foreseen by Nostradamus. But he was morally and politically opposed to the regime and it may have been his desire to discredit the Nazi hierarchy that prompted him, or his father, to suggest to Hess that he should take his chance to make peace while the planetary alignments were favourable. Ironically, it may have been Albrecht's ability to put a pro-Nazi spin on those same prophecies which saved his neck when he and his father were arrested by the Gestapo a few days after the capture of the Nazis' deputy leader because, after intensive questioning, they were allowed to leave.

Hitler's smouldering resentment at Hess's betrayal prompted the latter's replacement, Martin Bormann, to issue a decree on 9 June 1941, banning all forms of non-Aryan occultism. *Aktion Hess*, as it was called, saw hundreds of occult booksellers, fortune-tellers, complementary therapists, theosophists and the like dragged out of their beds in the early hours and interrogated by the Gestapo who considered such people subversive and a threat to the stability of the State. Many had their books, files and paranormal paraphernalia confiscated, but were allowed to go free after promising to cease their 'pagan' practices. However, there were those whose answers did not satisfy their interrogators or who were suspected of having advised the traitor, and they were subsequently imprisoned or sent to concentration camps from which they never emerged.

JAMES BOND AND THE BEAST

The story of Rudolf Hess's flight to Scotland reads like a chapter from a wartime thriller and that may be attributed to the fact that it could have been hatched by a master of the modern spy novel, Ian Fleming, creator of James Bond.

In the spring of 1941, Fleming was working for British Naval Intelligence who were planning to lure a top Nazi official to Britain under false pretences in order to prick the inflated collective Nazi ego, or so the story goes. It was decided that Hitler's Deputy, Rudolf Hess, was the most likely candidate to take the bait as he was known to be obsessed with astrology and might be suggestible. Fleming and his 'black ops' unit used an underground network of agents and sympathizers to feed Berlin the line that the Duke of Hamilton and a group of British aristocrats were plotting a coup against Churchill, but first needed to negotiate a secret peace deal with Germany. The lure was sweetened with the promise that 11 May 1941 was the most auspicious date for negotiations as it saw the conjunction of six planets in the constellation of Taurus with the added propitious influence of a full moon. Hess would have to act while the heavens were beckoning or miss his opportunity to ensure his place in history.

Unbelievably, Hess swallowed the story hook, line and sinker. Unfortunately for the British, however, they had landed a very odd fish indeed and decided not to exploit their great propaganda coup as much as they could have. Hess, it seemed, was *non compos mentis*, or as his Scottish captors would have said, 'two slices short of a full loaf'. Parading this wild-eyed captive in front of the newsreel cameras seemed tantamount to putting a lunatic on show. The army took a few frames to prove that they had indeed captured Hitler's second in command, then they locked him up while they debriefed him.

During the interrogation, at which Ian Fleming was present, Hess was said to have spoken in an unintelligible tongue which his interrogators suspected might be esoteric in nature. According to Fleming's biographer John Pearson in *The Life of Ian Fleming* (1966), the future author approached his immediate superior, Rear Admiral John Godfrey, and suggested that '[Aleister] Crowley should be allowed to interview Hess about the role of the occult in Nazism'. Fleming believed that Crowley might be able to press Hess to reveal the extent to which the Nazi hierarchy was under the influence of astrology, but it seems that others involved in the sting, most notably Fleming's friend, Maxwell Knight, were not happy to have such a shameless self-publicist in on the game. Pearson remarked:

'For many years [Fleming] had been fascinated by the legend of wickedness which had attached itself to the name of Aleister Crowley, necromancer, black magician and the Great Beast 666. This immensely ugly old diabolist and self-advertiser had thrown himself into certain more unsavoury areas of the occult with a gusto that must have appealed to Fleming, and when the interrogators from British Intelligence began trying to make sense of the neurotic and highly superstitious Hess he got the idea that

Crowley might be able to help and tracked him down to a place near Torquay, where he was living harmlessly on his own and writing patriotic poetry to encourage the war effort. He seems to have had no difficulty in persuading the old gentleman to put his gifts at the disposal of the nation.'

Crowley corresponded with Fleming on the matter.

'Sir: If it is true that Herr Hess is much influenced by astrology and Magick, my services might be of use to the Department in case he should not be willing to do what you wish. I have the honour to be, Sir, Your obedient servant, Aleister Crowley'

The self-styled 'Beast' attached a copy of his latest patriotic poem, 'England Stand Fast', which by all accounts had the boys of Naval Intelligence in stitches for days. For reasons never disclosed, this particular episode was omitted from the American edition of Fleming's biography. Undaunted by Maxwell Knight's refusal to allow him access to Hess, the notorious magician offered to collaborate with Intelligence to produce fake prophecies and other 'occult literature' to drop behind enemy lines to demoralize the, at the time, undefeated *Wehrmacht*. His offer was never taken up.

Incidentally, Crowley also claimed the credit for creating the 'V' for Victory sign which was adopted by Churchill and imitated by millions of soldiers and civilians during the war as a symbol of British defiance. Crowley explained that he took it from the magical sign for the gods 'Apophis and Typhon', while the equally popular 'thumbs up', which he also claimed to have introduced, was a magical sign for the god 'Khem'. Crowley also took delight in impressing dinner guests with his assurance that the fascist straight-arm 'Hitler salute' also had magical associations, being taken from a Golden Dawn ritual in which it represented the adept's acknowledgement of earth energy.

It is said that when Fleming was looking to create a suitable villain for his first Bond book, *Casino Royale* (1953), he recalled his encounter with Crowley. In the finished novel, the Crowley character, Le Chiffre (The Cipher), is described as 'very pale or white, fat, slug-like, with sadistic impulses, constantly using a benzedrine inhaler and with an insatiable appetite for women. He also had a rather feminine mouth.' One imagines that such a huge megalomaniac as Crowley would have been flattered to have been immortalized in such colourful terms.

HITLER AND 'THE BEAST'

'After five years of folly and weakness, miscalled politeness, tact, discretion, care for the feeling of others, I am weary of it. I say today; to hell with Christianity, Rationalism, Buddhism, all the lumber of the centuries. I bring you a positive and primeval fact, Magic by name; and with this I will build me a new Heaven and a new Earth. I want none of your faint

approval or your faint dispraise; I want blasphemy,
murder, rape, revolution, anything, bad or good, but
strong.'

Aleister Crowley

It is known that a German disciple of the notorious black
magician Aleister Crowley sent a copy of his infamous black
bible, *The Book of the Law*, to Hitler in 1925 or 1926, together
with a letter urging the future Führer to adopt its credo. As a
loyal acolyte of the 'Beast', Martha Kuntzel believed Crowley's
sex magick cult offered the means of self-realization and
the awakening of the Holy Guardian Angel, or True Self, in
contrast to orthodox religion which Crowley and his followers
rejected as constricting and dogmatic. This explains Kuntzel's
contradictory attitude to satanic magic in her advice to Hitler
as recorded by the reformed Nazi, Hermann Rauschning, in his
reminiscences, *Hitler Speaks* (1940).

'My Führer, don't touch black magic! As yet both white
and black are open to you. But once you've embarked
on black magic it will dominate your destiny. It will
hold you captive. Don't choose the quick and easy
successes. There lies before you the power of a realm
over pure spirits. Do not allow yourself to be led away
from your true path by earthbound spirits, which will
rob you of your creative power.'

The 'Great Beast', Aleister Crowley (1875–1947), in his robes of the Order of the Golden Dawn: the self-proclaimed 'wickedest man on earth' pitched in for Britain to help battle the Nazis.

Crowley was later to claim that his permissive belief system (itself a corruption of Rabelais' doctrine 'Do What Thou Will') had been adopted by the Nazi leader who was in the habit of quoting key passages from *The Book of the Law*, specifically Chapter l, verse 44 which Hitler paraphrased as: 'A new age of magic interpretation of the world is coming, of interpretation in terms of the will and not the intelligence.' And again from Chapter 11, verses 27–32 which Hitler paraphrased as: 'We are now at the end of the Age of Reason. The intellect has grown autocratic and become a disease of life.'

Shortly before the outbreak of the war, Martha Kuntzel wrote to Crowley agreeing that the parallels were either a shameless steal or at least an amazing 'coincidence', such as would occur if Hitler had tapped into the Universal Mind from which Crowley had taken his inspiration.

> '... *it began to dawn upon me how much of Hitler's thoughts were as if they had been taken from the Law of Thelema. I became his fervent admirer, and am so now, and will be to my end. I have ever so often owned to this firm conviction that the close identity of Hitler's ideas with what the Book teaches endowed me with the strength necessary for my work. I stated this even to the Gestapo some years ago.*'

But fanciful as it might seem that anyone could believe that Hitler might have adopted Crowley's muddled, self-indulgent philosophy – if indeed one was to suppose that he was even aware of Crowley's existence – there can be no denying that there are chilling parallels between Crowley's sixth-form nihilism and the Nazi *Weltanschauung*.

Chapter 11, verse 21 of *The Book of the Law* might have been taken directly from a speech by Hitler:

> *'We have nothing with the outcast and unfit: let them die in their misery. For they feel not. Compassion is the vice of kings, stamp down the wretched and the weak: this is the law of the strong: this is our law and the joy of the world.'*

CONVERSATIONS WITH THE BEAST

Hitler: *'And are you an angel of darkness?'*
Crowley: *'You'll find out in good time all about me. For the present, I'll say this: if I were an angel of light, you wouldn't want to know me.'*

unsubstantiated conversation attributed to Hitler and Crowley, from John Symonds' *The Medusa's Head* (1991)

Crowley's acolytes and his fiercest critics have been locked in a war of words concerning his alleged wartime activities ever since the self-styled 'Beast' hinted he might have been playing a double game – working for the Allies as an agent while playing devil's advocate to Hitler himself. Knowing the delight Crowley took in offending the easily offended and in shamelessly lying to enhance his already considerable reputation as 'the wickedest man in the world', it is likely that he was the sole source of these wild and unsubstantiated yarns. But the Allies would never have entrusted an incautious and irresponsible drug addict with sensitive information, while the Nazis would not have permitted such a larger-than-life character within 50 feet of their beloved Führer.

This argument, however, has failed to dampen the enthusiasm of Crowley's disciples. Occult author John Symonds has the self-styled Laird of Boleskin musing on his tête-à-tête with the Führer in his fictional biography of the 'Beast', *The Medusa's Head*.

> '*I never met ... someone as demonic as Herr Hitler. ... It is as if God said, "Let mankind learn a lesson; they need to open their eyes a little wider. Hitler will do that for them. Just wait. They will see things that men have never seen or heard before—such horrors that there will be no word in the German or any other language to describe them." That is what the demonic is when it appears in a very ordinary person, a man of the people, someone the intellectuals are contemptuous of but not the masses. With an uncanny instinct, they know who he is.*'

Those who believe that Hitler was a genuine black magician cite the scale of the genocide he perpetrated as evidence that he was making a sacrifice to the old gods just as the Sumerians had done millennia before. Hitler had made it known that he felt 'cheated of his war' by the Munich Agreement of September 1938 which gave him the Sudetenland and Czechoslovakia in return for more empty assurances, which suggests there was a satanic promise to be fulfilled rather than a political agenda. When Britain and France finally declared war on Germany in September 1940, the sky burned blood red over Berchtesgaden. All who witnessed it agreed that it was an evil portent for Germany.

PSYCHIC SELF-DEFENCE

While Crowley was offering his services to British Intelligence, or so he claimed, another English occultist was doing her bit for Britain on a higher plane. In 1940, Dion Fortune, an initiate of the Golden Dawn who founded the Fraternity of the Inner Light in the 1920s, presided over a magic circle in the mist-shrouded town of Glastonbury, the heart of Arthurian England.

Every Sunday lunchtime, they would sit 'in circle' and visualize national archetypes who would come to the aid of the nation to strengthen morale and meddle with Hitler's mind. Their energy was supplemented by emanations from members of the public who were invited to attend in spirit. Whether King Arthur, Merlin and St George were successfully invoked, no one knows, but Fortune was confident that her group had contributed to Hitler's decision to postpone Operation Sea Lion, the sea-borne invasion of Britain.

KING OF THE WITCHES

About the same time as Fortune was encouraging her followers to assist 'the few' during the summer of 1940, Gerald Gardner, the self-styled 'King of the Witches' and a close friend of Crowley, convened his coven at the sacred Rufus Stone in the New Forest to perform a rite of ceremonial magic. Its purpose was to erect a protective cone of 'astral light' around the embattled British Isles. It was not the first time such a rite had been performed. According to Gardner his pagan predecessors had fended off both Napoleon and the Spanish Armada using the same spells.

Traditionally, a sacrifice was required to make the work potent, but the ageing participants lacked the heart for a blood offering, so it was decided one of their number should perform the ritual 'skyclad', meaning naked, while the remainder stripped off and covered themselves in grease to protect themselves from the chill night air. The idea was that the unprotected soul would be expected to catch a cold and die of natural causes, thus saving the coven from the unwanted attentions of the British Bobby. But being elderly, not one but two succumbed and died within days. Mad though they might have been, it is a fact that shortly thereafter Hitler abandoned his plans to invade Britain and turned his attention eastwards instead.

BURN, WITCH, BURN

A year later in Ashdown Forest, Sussex, Crowley was putting his considerable knowledge of magic and showmanship into practice. He had invited a group of acolytes to the woods and formed them into two circles, one within the other. In the centre sat an effigy of Hitler dressed in a Nazi uniform. Crowley's coven were evidently in deadly earnest as they were all attired in ceremonial robes embossed with runic symbols like extras in a Hammer horror film. As the members circled the dummy, they intoned the 'barbarous words of power' to bind the effigy with its mortal counterpart across the Channel. Then came the climax of the affair when the dummy was fitted with wings, hoisted to the top of a local church and set ablaze. Before the spire could catch alight, it was cut free and launched towards Berlin.

HIMMLER'S 'PET ASTROLOGER'

Among the ragged collective of soothsayers, palmists and wild-eyed prophets netted by the Gestapo and thrown into Fuhlsbüttel concentration camp in the wake of *Aktion Hess* was an ex-member of the Berlin psychics group, the 'Swastika Circle', with a reputation for uncannily accurate astrological forecasts and a compulsion to caricature those he despised. In the summer of 1923, Wilhelm Wulff had plotted the charts of Hitler, Goering and SA leader Ernst Röhm and warned all who would listen that, if they hitched their star to that of the future Führer, they would share his fate. Hitler, said Wulff, was destined to be feared and to 'issue cruel and senseless orders' which would lead to his self-destruction shortly before May 1945. History proved him to be correct. Röhm was slain in a bloody purge of the SA leadership known as 'the

Night of the Long Knives' in 1934, Hitler was to commit suicide in the bunker beneath Berlin on 30 April and Goering cheated the hangman by swallowing cyanide in his cell in Nuremberg in 1945.

Of course, it did not take a seer to foretell that the Hitler gang was likely to invoke the old adage forecasting disaster for those who lived by the sword, but Wulff was fairly specific regarding dates, particularly those relating to the various attempts that would be made on the Führer's life and his numerous psychosomatic disorders.

PENDULUM AND PENTAGRAM

On his release from Fuhlsbüttel in March 1942, Wulff was instructed to report to an ultra-secret institute attached to the naval headquarters in Berlin where he was to be employed as a research assistant. However, on his arrival he was shocked to learn the real nature of this department and the duties he was expected to perform.

'... *the National Socialist leaders proposed to use these 'research centres' to harness, not only natural, but supernatural, forces. All intellectual, natural and supernatural sources of power – from modern technology to medieval black magic, and the teachings of Pythagoras to the Faustian pentagram incantation – were to be exploited in the interests of final victory.'*

This occult 'think tank' was run by a naval officer who must have been tempted to put in for a transfer to the Russian front when he found he was overseeing the activities of spiritualist mediums, pendulum practitioners, astrologers and 'sensitives', all of whom had their gifts put to practical use in the service of the Reich. The seers were put to work divining the location of Allied shipping, using little more than a pendulum suspended over a chart of the Atlantic. 'The results were, of course, pitiful,' Wulff recalled, betraying a hint of snobbery and the belief that his 'rivals' were no match for esoteric astrology. 'Whatever one may think about occult phenomena, it was simply ridiculous to expect that an unknown world could be forcibly opened up in this dilettante fashion and exploited for military purposes. Even in those cases where there was some initial success, no attempt was made to evaluate the findings by systematic scientific procedures.'

The most convincing evidence for the efficacy of divination had been made the previous year by a 60-year-old retired architect by the name of Ludwig Straniak, who told his superiors that if he were to be shown a photograph of a ship he could pinpoint its position on a map with his pendulum. Their incredulity evaporated when he successfully located both the *Bismarck* and the *Prinz Eugen*, ships which the British had been hunting unsuccessfully for months. However, even that remarkable achievement wasn't sufficient to convince the sceptical military minds that Straniak would be an asset to the Reich. Back at the naval institute, he was presented with a unique test. A lump of metal was placed on a large piece of paper and then removed.

Straniak was then brought into the room and asked to scan the paper with his pendulum and state where the metal had been. Again he was successful.

Unfortunately, those in charge did not understand the nature of psychic sensitivity and put enormous pressure on Straniak and his colleagues to produce results on which the U-boat wolf packs could act. Inevitably, the group members succumbed to the stress of having to prove themselves day after day and their potency declined rapidly as if their psychic batteries were being drained. Straniak's health deteriorated and his colleagues were dismissed. The institute returned to conventional scientific experiments.

Ironically, German Naval Intelligence had been keen to persevere with the 'occult bureau' in the belief that the British were doing the same. How else could they account for Allied success in tracking and sinking so many U-boats? In fact, although the Allies were experimenting with similar techniques, their success was purely due to them having cracked the German secret 'Enigma' code, a fact that remained unknown to the enemy until long after the war.

Despite his obvious lack of enthusiasm for Project Pendulum, Wulff's paymasters were sufficiently impressed with his esoteric credentials and his accuracy to commission him to devise a Zen Buddhist-style psychic 'brainwashing' programme to harden the German soldier in mind and body in preparation for the privations he was expected to endure during the invasion of Russia later that same year, and to instil in each man the need for self-sacrifice. They were convinced that the Japanese had instilled fanatical zeal in their soldiers by a combination of psychological indoctrination and drugs and they were seriously considering conditioning the SS troops in the same way. No one knows if Wulff did as he was asked, but it is a fact that the SS spearhead earned a reputation for almost suicidal self-sacrifice during their initial assault on Russia that autumn.

THE BUDDHA OF BERLIN

It was Wulff's activities at the Naval Institute which brought him, one crisp winter's evening in 1942, to the attention of Himmler's masseur and personal physician Felix Kersten, a grotesquely corpulent, waxy-skinned man with 'greedy eyes' and 'grasping hands' – if Wulff's description is to be believed. Kersten was an obvious quack, but he had wallowed in the shallows of pseudo-science long enough to distinguish a serious astrologer from a common fortune-teller. In his elegant apartment on the Rudesheimer Platz in Berlin, forcibly acquired from its former owner, Kersten squatted like a sullen Buddha and inquired what conclusions Wulff had drawn from Hitler's horoscope. As the astrologer was later to claim in his autobiography, *Zodiac and Swastika* (1973), he pointed out certain ominous alignments.

> *'I then suggested that a man like Hitler could not be a successful national leader for long. I foresaw bitter events which were bound to occur unless there was a radical*

change of policy. At that time the Moscow and Leningrad offensive had been broken off and our troops were engaged in "strategic" withdrawals which were actually to last three long years. I told Kersten that Hitler had the same Saturn position in his natal chart as Napoleon and that, although their destinies were not identical, there were certain parallels, applying primarily to Germany's Russian campaign and the battles still to come.'

Wulff suggested that, if Germany were to be saved from total defeat and destruction, something would have to be done soon and implied that Kersten took the hint.

'I then went on to say that my negative forecast for Hitler's personal future was borne out by mundane horoscopes, especially the horoscope for Germany and the chart for January 30, 1933 – i.e., the founding of the Third Reich.'

Kersten appears to have taken his guest's assessment seriously. Wulff had singled himself out by his mastery of Sidereal Astrology, a more esoteric branch of the art which had originated in India thousands of years earlier and which was considered to be far more accurate than the western system as it is based on the precise position of the planets and the luminaries in relation to the Ecliptic (the great circle on the celestial sphere representing the annual path of the Sun) rather than the Tropical (either of the two parallel circles on the celestial sphere having the same latitudes and names as the corresponding lines on Earth), as is the case in Western astrology. More significantly, this Hindu tradition did not contradict Nazi ideology which refused to admit that an Aryan and an *Untermensch* (racially inferior individual) could share the same destiny.

In order to study the system, Wulff had acquired a working knowledge of Sanskrit which impressed Kersten, the would-be mystic, but Kersten jealously guarded his access to Himmler and was not willing to relinquish his place at the trough. In order to ensure Wulff's subservience and gratitude, Kersten set himself up as Wulff's sponsor, commissioning projections for the SS inner circle which he would insist on approving before presenting at an opportune moment to the Reichsführer SS.

DINING WITH THE DEVIL

Wulff might have remained an obscure minor figure in the Nazi psychological warfare machine had he not contributed to the audacious rescue of Hitler's closest ally, Benito Mussolini. The Italian dictator had been deposed by rivals in the Fascist Grand Council on 24 July 1943 and imprisoned on the Island of Ponza, less than 75 miles (120 kilometres) south-east of Rome by supporters of his successor, Marshal Badoglio.

Within days, Himmler ordered the SS Intelligence Service to locate Mussolini using every variety of 'occult science' at their disposal. This prompted the Gestapo to round up the most reliable astrologers and radiesthesists (pendulum diviners) in the

Reich for a top secret summit at Wannsee, where they were plied with food and drink and ordered to identify the location within 24 hours – or face the consequences.

Wulff offered a different version of these events in his autobiography. He claimed to have been the only astrologer to have been consulted and added that he produced the required answer within hours. However, before Mussolini could be rescued, he was moved to a mountain prison in Gran Sasso from which he was later liberated by German paratroopers. Whatever the truth of the matter, Wulff's contribution had been duly noted and as a reward for his services he received a personal invitation to dine with SS General Artur Nebe at the Kaiserhof Hotel in Berlin.

While most of the civilian population of war-torn Europe scavenged for scraps, Nebe and his guest gorged themselves on cognac and American cigarettes until the topic of conversation turned to great men and their horoscopes. Wulff tactlessly remarked that, according to his calculations Adolf Hitler would share the same destiny as Napoleon, Cromwell and Wallenstein, the 17th-century German general and statesman, but Nebe let the prediction pass, possibly because he shared Wulff's vision of the future.

Before he could take Wulff into his confidence, Nebe put him to the test by presenting him with two sets of anonymous biographies from which he was to sketch a basic chart on the spot. The first was said to be that of a criminal and the second, a spy. In fact, they were for Nebe and his sidekick, Loebbe.

Summing up the prospects for the man designated as the 'spy', Wulff remarked that he had 'moderate gifts as a detective' which must have amused his host. But his prognosis for 'the criminal' left Nebe visibly shaken. 'You don't need to bother too much about this man,' Wulff told him. 'He'll soon fall into the hands of the Kriminalpolizei and will come to a violent end.'

Unbeknown to Wulff, Nebe had in fact been playing a double game, working secretly with the July plotters, presumably in the hope of saving his own skin by joining the anti-Hitler faction before the Allies could win the war and put him on trial. When the assassination attempt failed, the SS rounded up the conspirators and executed them by hanging them from meat hooks with piano wire wound round their necks. Nebe managed to evade capture for months, but was eventually betrayed and executed by his own men, just as Wulff predicted, on 4 March 1945. Having passed the test, Wulff left his host later that evening with orders to produce detailed charts and analyses for two dozen high-ranking Nazi officials who were suspected of corruption. He had entered the serpent's lair.

MEETING HIMMLER

In the spring of 1944, Wulff penetrated deeper into the shadowy world of the Reichsführer SS when he encountered Himmler's trusted lieutenant, Walter Schellenberg, the shy, softly spoken officer in charge of counter-espionage at the Reich Central Security Office. If the astrologer's account is to be believed,

Schellenberg quizzed Wulff on the more questionable aspects of astrology and, having satisfied himself on this account, shared his most intimate thoughts concerning the forced removal of Hitler from his office and from this Earth. Wulff replied, 'Unfortunately, Hitler's removal would not change the course of events.'

> 'Far too much has happened for that. I have been studying Hitler's horoscope for twenty years now. I have a pretty clear idea of what is ultimately in store for him. He will probably die under the hand of an assassin, certainly in 'Neptunian' – that is, enigmatic – circumstances, in which a woman will play a leading part. The world will probably never know the precise details of his death, for in Hitler's horoscope Neptune has long been in bad aspect to other planets. Moreover, Neptune is extremely strong in his horoscope, and it was always to be expected that his great military projects would have a dubious outcome.'

Wulff concluded that the astrological prospects for Britain and America were extremely advantageous at that moment and would peak in mid-May 1945. Action would have to be taken, he said, if Germany was to avoid 'greater misfortunes'.

Unbeknown to Wulff, Himmler was already planning the downfall of his Führer, but he was crippled by indecision and doubt. The one thing that might persuade him to act on his daydreams was a favourable sign from the stars. News of Wulff's intimate conversations with Nebe and Schellenberg reached him at a critical time and he issued a summons for the astrologer to be brought to him at Bergwald, his own private castle at Aigen near Salzburg. Himmler was then on a fatless and meatless diet due to a digestive disorder, but as he and Wulff exchanged pleasantries at the luncheon table the Reichsführer confessed that he hated the sight of blood and could not bear to witness the suffering of an animal. These words seem obscene, coming from the man who was directly responsible for the cold-blooded butchery of millions of innocent men, women and children.

Wulff noted that Himmler had a pallid complexion and red eyelids – indicative of overwork – and a cruel, cynical mouth, although he had greeted his guest cordially and appeared to enjoy conversation as long as the subject was to his liking. After lunch, Wulff was invited to a private audience with Himmler in his large but sparsely furnished study overlooking the grounds framed by the lilac-blue mountains of Obersalzberg. The Reichsführer began by enthusing on astrology and occult matters, confiding to his guest that he was in the habit of consulting a lunar calendar before embarking on important projects. He also defended the recently implemented policy which forbade anyone to practise astrology without the regime's approval.

For his part Wulff attempted to make the distinction between astrology and fortune-telling, but Himmler proved both opinionated and inflexible. The Reichsführer explained:

'We base our attitude on the fact that astrology, as a universalist doctrine, is diametrically opposed to our own *philosophical view of the world. Astrologers claim to be able to cast horoscopes for the entire globe, for the whole of humanity. But it is precisely this that we National Socialists and SS members are obliged to reject out of hand. A doctrine which is meant to apply in equal measure to Negroes, Indians, Chinese and Aryans is in crass opposition to our conception of the racial soul. Each one of the peoples I have named has its own specific racial soul, just as we have ours and consequently no one doctrine can cover all cases.'*

It was clear from the technical terms Himmler dropped into their conversation that he possessed a working knowledge of astrology and was familiar with astrological expressions such as trine aspects, positive and negative signs and the elevation of planets. 'He was acquainted with the fundamental principles of a horoscope,' Wulff observed, 'and knew how to apply them.' But Wulff was struck by Himmler's political naivety and the shallowness of his personality.

'[He] asked me the strangest and most infantile questions in his quest for astrological enlightenment about the military and political situation. God knows, Himmler was no genius. Rather, he was a mediocrity, especially when you saw him in private ... He was a pettifogging bureaucrat with scruples.'

As Hitler's 1000-year Reich neared its own *Gotterdämmerung*, Himmler came to rely more and more on his 'pet astrologer', having convinced himself that Wulff possessed a genuine gift for prophecy. On 9 December 1944, the Reichsführer had narrowly escaped death as Wulff had predicted he would on that day.

> *'"It's a strange thought, isn't it, Herr Wulff," said Himmler breaking off from a discourse on the subject of loyalty and honour which he considered uniquely German qualities, "that on December 9th I actually had an accident which might well have proved fatal. I was driving at night and 130 feet above the Black Forest railway, I ran off the road and down the hill on to the tracks just as a train was approaching. We only just managed to get out of the way in time. The accuracy of your horoscope is phenomenal."'*

During these last months of the war as the Allies encircled the demoralized remnants of the German army, the Reichsführer repeatedly turned in desperation to Wulff and demanded to know what options the stars offered for his survival. Wulff dutifully consulted the natal charts of those involved on both sides and armed with the requisite data urged Himmler to have the courage of his convictions and act to overthrow Hitler as Schellenberg and Kersten had been urging him to do for months.

But yet again Himmler's dithering and indecisiveness proved his undoing. By the time he had finally committed himself to a plan, all escape routes had been cut off. On 22 May 1945, he was captured by the British dressed as an NCO with an eye patch, carrying false documents in the name of 'Heinrich Hitzinger'. While in custody, he committed suicide by swallowing cyanide. The best Wulff could say of Himmler, one of the most feared men in history, was that he was true to his flag and his oath of allegiance to his leader. 'His only other saving grace was economy. When it came to finances, he balanced his books down to the last pfennig.'

HITLER AND ASTROLOGY

The smokescreen of propaganda and popular myth has obscured the true extent to which the Nazi hierarchy were obsessed with astrology and dependent upon their seers for advice.

Hitler could be said to have had an ambivalent attitude towards the subject – he approved of it when it appeared to endorse his plans, but dismissed it out of hand when it contradicted his own instincts. He appears to have professed a passing interest mainly to appease Himmler, who refused to make a single significant decision without recourse to his own personal astrological advisor, but the Führer distrusted anyone who relied on the stars to dictate their destiny.

After the war his private secretary, Christa Schroeder, attempted to downplay the Führer's reported obsession with the stars. She told journalist Albert Zoller, author of *Hitler in Private* (1949):

'There were popular rumours that Hitler allowed himself to be guided by astrologers before reaching any important

decision. I must confess that I never noticed anything of the kind and the subject was never mentioned in conversation. On the contrary, Hitler refuted this by his firmly held conviction that people born on the same day, at the same place and at the same hour, in no way had the same fate. For this viewpoint he thought that twins provided the best evidence. He always vigorously rejected the proposition that the fate of individuals depends upon their stars or constellations.'

This view had been contradicted by Himmler who told Wulff: 'We cannot permit any astrologers to follow their calling except those who are working for us. In the National Socialist state astrology must remain a *privilegium singulorum*. It is not for the broad masses ...' By this it is understood he was making a distinction between those who practised the esoteric science of astrology in service to the state and common fortune-tellers.

While Hitler may have been inclined to consult astrologers before making a major decision – at least before he began to believe in his own infallibility – for his loyal lieutenant Heinrich Himmler, astrology was the guiding principle of life. His dependency on portents and prophecies was a source of wry amusement among the more sceptical members of the regime. Hitler's blue-eyed protégé, Reinhard Heydrich, once summed it up by saying: 'Goering is worried about the stars on his chest, Himmler about those in his horoscope.'

Sentries stand guard at the Ehrentempel, two 'temples' in Munich designed by Paul Ludwig Troost to honour the 'victims' of the failed 1923 putsch. Troost's death in 1934 was taken by Hitler as a bad omen for the regime.

ADOLF HITLER'S DREAM

Hitler may not have been a fervent believer in astrology, but he was extremely superstitious by nature. A prophetic dream during the First World War which saved him from almost certain death was only one of several incidents which convinced the Führer that his life was protected by providence and that it confirmed he had a divine mission to fulfil.

During a lull in the fighting on the Western Front in 1917, Corporal Hitler, a runner in the Bavarian Infantry, fell asleep at his post. Minutes later he awoke in a distressed state having dreamt he had been buried alive after a shell had exploded in the trench. He scrambled to his feet clutching at his chest which had been hit by smouldering shrapnel in the dream. When he finally came to his senses and saw that he was actually unharmed, he became aware that his comrades were also unhurt and had returned to cleaning their weapons and playing cards, having shrugged off Hitler's panic as just another case of battle fatigue. It was then that he felt compelled to leave the dugout and venture out across no man's land, despite the risk of being shot by an enemy sniper.

At the moment he realized the great danger in which he had put himself, a roaring sound overhead made him throw himself instinctively into a shell crater, then a tremendous explosion shook the ground, showering him with mud and debris.

When he finally recovered his nerve, he scrambled back to the trench where he found his dead comrades buried under mounds of earth and shattered metal just as he had foreseen in his dream. Hitler was the sole survivor. [Source: Stuart Holdroyd, *Psychic Voyages*, Aldus Publishing, 1977]

In another incident which happened many years later, in October 1933, Hitler was delighted to be invited to lay the foundation stone of the House of German Art in Munich which had been designed by his close personal friend, Paul Ludwig Troost. However, when Hitler struck the stone at the dedication ceremony, the hammer shattered in his hand.

For months afterwards he brooded on what had happened and he considered it to be an ill omen. It was only when Troost fell seriously ill and later died (in January 1934) that Hitler felt that the black cloud had been lifted from around his head.

'When that hammer shattered I knew at once it was an evil omen,' he told his architect, Albert Speer. 'Something is going to happen I thought. Now we know why the hammer broke. The architect was destined to die.'

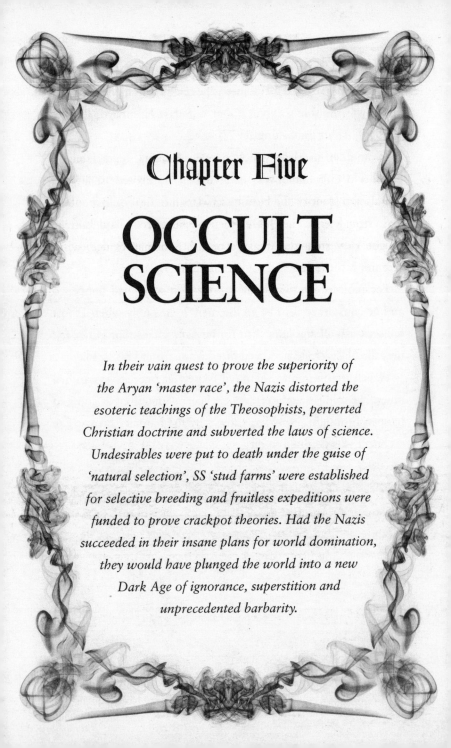

Chapter Five

OCCULT SCIENCE

In their vain quest to prove the superiority of
the Aryan 'master race', the Nazis distorted the
esoteric teachings of the Theosophists, perverted
Christian doctrine and subverted the laws of science.
Undesirables were put to death under the guise of
'natural selection', SS 'stud farms' were established
for selective breeding and fruitless expeditions were
funded to prove crackpot theories. Had the Nazis
succeeded in their insane plans for world domination,
they would have plunged the world into a new
Dark Age of ignorance, superstition and
unprecedented barbarity.

The Nazis believed that if they captured the spiritual centre of a country, their enemy would lose their will to resist and capitulate. The same would be true if its symbols of power were taken, its regimental flags, icons of cultural identity and crown jewels. The enemy would sense that its national identity had been lost and its morale would crumble.

So from Vienna they looted the Hapsburg crown jewels, from Prague they stole the treasure of the Bohemian kings, while Warsaw lost the Polish royal regalia to the Reich. In his defence, Hitler cited the precedent established by the Emperor Napoleon and by the British who had presented the sacred Koh-i-Noor diamond to Queen Victoria for whom it was no more than a very expensive bauble.

Hitler had been a vociferous critic of the monarchy and the aristocracy which he derided as 'a classic example of the laws of selective breeding operating in reverse'. Royal families became more degenerate with each generation, he asserted, until their members succumbed to insanity. Nature, argued Hitler, supported his belief in the Führer principle, the ascension of those who had proven their fitness to rule. For this reason he regarded the emblems of royalty with disdain, but he understood their symbolic value, conferring power and authority on those courageous enough to claim them.

SACRED SITES

The origin of the Nazi belief that each nation possesses a sacred centre, and that to possess it is to subjugate its people, was a distortion of the laws of the esoteric science of geomancy. The ancients believed that certain locations were sources of psychic energy and that this force could be drawn upon for communicating with the forces of nature and the gods. For this reason they built their megalithic monuments and temples over underground streams, near natural magnetic fields or at the point of converging leylines, all of which could be divined by the community's priests and shamans. The practice extended across Europe, India and Asia. The ancient Chinese, for example, adopted the idea in their development of acupuncture, which operates on the principle that the human body, too, has a network of invisible energy lines that can be mapped and the flow of etheric energy unblocked or diverted by the insertion of needles at key points.

The Nazi fascination with sacred sites can be traced back to the theories of a British antiquarian, William Henry Black, who in 1870 first proposed the idea that many of the world's ancient monuments conformed to a grand geometrical pattern, perhaps coincidentally rather than by design. However, the fact that these sacred stone circles and temples were located at the focal point of a natural energy source suggested that early civilizations and communities may not have been as primitive as 19th-century science had assumed they were.

Between the wars the idea found enthusiastic support among amateur antiquarians in Germany who discovered that the distances between many monolithic structures revealed that their ancestors possessed a remarkably sophisticated understanding of mathematics and astronomy. Willibrod Kirfel's

The Cosmology of the Indies (1921) argued convincingly that Aryan tribes in India had developed a complex cosmology which they had documented in stone at their most sacred sites. The following year, Otto Reuter galvanized the German academic establishment with *The Riddle of the Edda* which legitimized the beliefs of the eccentric *völkisch* occultists by demonstrating that there may have been a historic basis for the Norse myths. Reuter argued that there was a hitherto unknown Indo-European culture which had encoded their knowledge of the constellations in their creation myths. Then, in 1929, Wilhelm Teudt published his exhaustive study of the subject, *Ancient German Sanctuaries*, drawing on years of painstaking research and thousands of detailed measurements which he had personally made at sites throughout Germany. He claimed to have identified a national astronomical cult based on 'extensive scientific foundations' which cemented the growing belief among mystically minded German nationalists that the Aryans were far more civilized than their non-Aryan counterparts in Africa and elsewhere. Teudt wrote:

'We have to unlearn our belief that the Roman Church under the Frankish Emperor Charles brought civilisation to the barbaric tribes of Germany. The old picture of our ancestors; primitive and incomprehensible customs, stunted, defiant and wild figures, ragged, scanty clothing of badly worked skins ... [gives way to] familiar solemn behaviour, the well-cared-for appearance of people at a

The crown jewels of the Hapsburg dynasty, the alleged source of their spiritual power.

fete, in elegant, properly made outfits, including well-tailored linen, woollen and hempen cloth. Sumptuous furs, rich jewellery of gold, silver, amber and bronze. Lively, expressive, melodious singing from which our best and most familiar folk songs come down to us, accompanied by technically-accomplished, sweet-sounding instruments.'

In such innocence and idealism the myth of the Master Race began to take shape supported by the specious new science of Eugenics (selective breeding).

VRIL POWER

In the 1920s, Josef Heinsch, a lawyer from Westphalia, discovered that many of the major leylines around the world originated under mountains and hills that had been deemed sacred as the dwelling places of the gods. Such sites were said to be sources of an all-powerful natural energy which could be harnessed by magical means.

Legend had it that the pagan priests of ancient Britain used it to reduce their enemies to ashes, which led to it being known as 'the lightning of the druids'. The Nazi mystics renamed it *vril*, adopting the name from *The Coming Race*, a novel by the British occult author and adept Bulwer-Lytton. Indeed, the force itself was not, it seems, an entirely fictional creation. During the same decade that Heinsch was tracing the source of the leylines, two scientists from Stuttgart were attempting to find a common factor linking cases of cancer in the city. H. Winzer and W. Melzer thought that there might be a geological basis for instances of the disease, but could find nothing until dowsers demonstrated that the cases were clustered around the region's five major underground fault lines.

When Nazi scientists were commissioned to follow up this research, they discovered that the velocity of the radiation that they detected by dowsing travelled at a median rate of 44 metres per second (98 mph), which was the same number as the Germanic geomantic measure, the *raste*. It appeared that there might be a link between the magnetic radiation emitted by the earth at ancient sacred sites and the standard unit of measurement used by the ancient astronomical cults in the construction of their sacred sites.

The potential power to be unleashed by those who desired to focus such a force can be gleaned from a description given in 1895 by A.P. Sinnett, a member of the London Theosophical Society, whose members were fervent believers in the existence of such forces.

'There are great etheric currents sweeping over the surface of the earth from pole to pole in volume which makes their power as irresistible as the rising tide: and there are methods by which this stupendous force may be safely utilised, though skilful attempts to control it would be fraught with frightful danger.'

When Heinrich Himmler learned of such a force, he determined that Germany would be the first to control it. And if the Nazis were to be judged by their deeds, it was clear it would not be used for the benefit of humanity.

THE WORLD OF ICE

'I shall construct ... an observatory in which will be represented the three great cosmological conceptions of history – those of Ptolemy, Copernicus and Hörbiger.'

Adolf Hitler, 28 April 1942

While geomancy continues to stimulate serious discussion in the 21st century as part of the New Age sciences, its more bizarre companions, the World Ice Theory and the Hollow Earth, elicit nothing but derision. But during the Hitler years, in the vacuum created by the defection of Einstein and the intellectual elite, they threatened to supplant mainstream science in the Nazi state.

Practitioners of esoteric disciplines from Ayurveda to Zen have a saying, 'Like attracts like', which they cite as one of the Universal Laws. It means that like-minded souls attract those who will aid them in their spiritual development, while those with a dark purpose will gravitate towards others of a similar nature. It was certainly true of the Nazis who attracted the scientists and philosophers they deserved – cranks and oddballs with the most outlandish theories imaginable.

Austrian engineer Hans Hörbiger (1860–1931) was typical of the eccentric pseudo-scientists who were sponsored by the state. And, in turn, he learned from them the power of threats and intimidation. In 1925, he recruited Nazi thugs to disrupt meetings and lectures held by orthodox physicists and he wrote threatening letters to the scientific publications and academics who disagreed with him. 'The time has come for you to choose,' he wrote, 'whether to be with us or against us. While Hitler is cleaning up politics, Hans Hörbiger will sweep the bogus sciences out of the way. The doctrine of Eternal Ice will be a sign of the regeneration of the German people. Watch out! Come over to our side before it is too late.'

The core of Hörbiger's theory was that the solar system was formed millions of years ago when a massive block of ice collided with the sun. The resulting explosion threw molten matter into space which eventually cooled to form the planets. He had come to this conclusion after witnessing the violent reaction caused by molten metal being poured on to snow in the foundry where he had worked. According to Hörbiger, this cosmic accident accounted for the existence of the poles and the Great Flood which was mythologized in the Bible and the Nordic legends of the *Edda*. But what really intrigued the mystically minded Nazis was the idea that the *Welteislehre* (World Ice Theory) offered a scientific basis for their belief in an antediluvian age of supermen which its proponent explained had been made possible by gravitational changes caused by one of the three moons orbiting the Earth.

Cover of the 1920s German occult magazine, Der Spiritismus *(Spiritualism)*.
Magazines such as this one flourished during the uncertain Weimar period
following defeat in the First World War.

Its increasing proximity resulted in a mutant race of giants who were rendered almost extinct when the moon finally collided with our planet 150,000 years ago, leaving their humanoid slaves scavenging for survival. The few remaining giants established several advanced civilizations, including the islands of Atlantis and Lemuria for a superior race of human beings, with the Aryans, whom they nurtured as their successors before being hunted down by their vengeful slaves, giving rise to the myths and legends of gods and heroes with which we are familiar today. It only remained for the Nazis to implement a selective breeding programme from pure Aryan stock to regenerate the race of Aryan supermen and restore them to their rightful place as rulers of the Earth. However, it was never satisfactorily explained how the regular-sized Aryans had inherited the blood from their oversized mentors.

When challenged to explain this and other glaring anomalies in his cosmology by practitioners of 'Jewish-Liberal science' (i.e., conventional science), such as the fact that the light-reflective capacity of the moon is lower than that of ice, Hörbiger had a typical Nazi retort: 'Trust me, not equations! When will you learn that mathematics is valueless.'

It is not known when Hitler was converted to Hörbiger's Aryan fantasy, but there is evidence that he was willing to act upon it. He is reputed to have said in January 1942:

'Nothing prevents us from supposing that mythology is a reflection of things that have existed and of which humanity

has retained a vague memory. In all the human traditions, whether oral or written, one finds mention of a huge cosmic disaster. What the Bible tells on the subject is not peculiar to the Jews, but was certainly borrowed by them from the Babylonians and Assyrians. In the Nordic legend we read of a struggle between gods and giants ... the thing is only explicable upon the hypothesis of a disaster that completely destroyed a humanity which already possessed a high degree of civilisation. The fragments of our prehistory are perhaps merely reproductions of objects belonging to a more distant past ... What proof have we ... that besides objects made of stone there were not similar objects made of metal? The life of bronze is limited ... Besides, there's no proof that the civilisation that existed before the disaster flourished precisely in our regions ... Who knows what discoveries will be made if we could explore the lands that are now covered by water?

'I'm quite inclined to accept the cosmic theories of Hörbiger. It's not impossible, in fact, that 10,000 years before our era there was a clash between the Earth and the Moon that gave the Moon its present orbit. It's also possible that the earth attracted to itself the atmosphere of the Moon and that this radically altered the conditions of life on our planet ... It seems to me that these questions will be capable of solution on the day when a man will intuitively establish the connection between these facts, thus teaching exact science the path to follow.'

Himmler became an ardent supporter of *Welteislehre* in the 1920s and remained so throughout the war. He is recorded as saying, 'Hans Hörbiger's monument does not need to wait a hundred years before it is built; one can employ these ideas even today.'

Unfortunately for the Nazis, Hitler did just that. In the late summer of 1941 he ordered the Central Army Group to halt within sight of the spires of Moscow while several mechanized divisions broke off in an ill-fated effort to capture Leningrad and another raced towards the oil fields of the Ukraine. When the snow began to fall in the first week of October, the former Bohemian corporal, now Supreme Commander of Germany's armed forces, shrugged off warnings that his troops were not prepared for a Russian winter by saying that he would 'take care of it'. It is assumed that he meant that he had faith in the meteorological department of the *Ahnenerbe* who had forecast an uncharacteristically mild winter using Hörbiger's principles and predictions. If so, it was a fatal error. Within weeks the vanguard of the German Army found itself in the pincer-like grip of a bitter Russian winter, kitted out in thin summer uniforms without gloves, hats, boots or even dark glasses to protect its members from snow blindness. The German newsreels made light of the situation, filming naked soldiers braving ice-water baths, but the reality was far grimmer. By early November the lubricating oil was freezing in their guns and synthetic fuel was separating into its component parts in the petrol tanks of their trucks and tanks.

By Christmas, one million of Germany's finest troops – the same men who had marched proudly down the Champs Elysées after the fall of France just two years earlier – perished in the snow, their weapons welded to their frozen fingers.

Hitler was shaken, but unrepentant. His belief in his own infallibility could not countenance defeat. Fate had conspired against him. He was right. Hörbiger had been right. Providence was testing his resolve. The Master Race must be forged anew in a trial of fire and ice, the two elements which formed the world aeons ago. He ordered the encircled 6th Army at Stalingrad to stand and fight to the last man, but even the most ardent Nazis found their resolve crystallizing in the sub-zero temperatures. On February 2 1943, after weeks of bitter hand-to-hand fighting the remnants of Field Marshall Bock's Army surrendered to the Russians, many never to see the Fatherland again.

A curious postscript to this story occurred in 1943 when Hitler inexplicably ordered the cessation of the top secret V2 rocket project. He is said to have had a dream in which he saw his potentially war-winning weapon shatter huge shards of ice floating above the Earth, bringing them crashing down and triggering a cosmic catastrophe. By the time Hitler had been persuaded that the rockets posed no danger to the world he wanted to conquer, it was too late to pursue his technological advantage. The war was lost.

THE HOLLOW EARTH

No one would accuse Reichsmarschall Hermann Goering of being an idealistic fool, not even behind his broad back.

Nonetheless, it is a fact that he subscribed to a concept even more outlandish than Hörbiger's World Ice Theory, one which would not have been out of place in a Jules Verne novel – the notion of the Hollow Earth.

The idea dates back to the 17th century when English astronomer Edmund Halley, the discoverer of the comet which bears his name, published a paper in which he postulated a theory to explain the variance of the Earth's magnetic poles. He envisaged the Earth's crust as the outer layer of a hollow sphere within which two inner layers spun at different speeds. The poles were supposedly situated on one or both of these inner layers and the variation in speed between the revolving spheres accounted for the variance in the cardinal points from day to day (the North-South-East-West alignment).

Three hundred years later, a variation on this idea was embraced by a former First World War German fighter ace and friend of Goering, by the name of Peter Bender. Bender must have suffered from shell shock because his premise clearly borders on the insane. He believed that the human race is living inside a large sphere, that the sky is its inner skin and that the stars are no more than glimmers of light seen through the holes in this greater sphere. He called this ludicrous notion 'the phantom universe' and, incredible as it might seem, Goering was not the only high-ranking Nazi to give it a veneer of credibility – many German naval officers accepted it too. In April 1942, a group headed by Dr Heinz Fischer succeeded in commissioning a full-scale test in the Baltic where a prototype radar station was established and

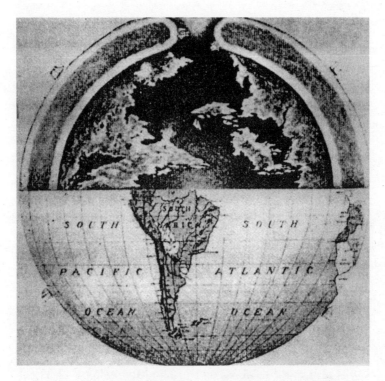

The 'Hollow Earth' theory, proposed by Peter Bender and put to the test by Dr Heinz Fischer, was even more outlandish than Hörbiger's World Ice Theory.

equipped to send beams of infra-red light up to the sky at an angle of 45 degrees. The hope was that the rays would bounce off the roof of the larger sphere back down to Earth where they would produce a radar image of ships that would be out of visual range of the vessel conducting the experiment: in this case the target was the British fleet anchored at Scapa Flow in the Orkney Islands. Needless to say, the experiment was a failure and the expedition returned to face the wrath of the Führer who considered the venture a serious waste of men and resources at a critical moment in the war. Bender and the most vociferous advocates of his theory were despatched to concentration camps. Even Goering was too embarrassed to speak in his friend's defence. Only Dr Fischer escaped with his life. After the war he was taken to America where he became a significant contributor to the development of the hydrogen bomb.

THE REAL RAIDERS OF THE LOST ARK

'My ancestors were pagans. My forebears were heretics.'

Otto Rahn

When the frozen body of SS Obersturmführer Otto Rahn (1904–39) was discovered on Kufstein Mountain on 13 March 1939, the assumption was that he had died of exposure after falling, or losing his way, in a blizzard. But, as his friend Paul Ladame observed, it would take up to two weeks to die of cold at that altitude at that time of the year. Besides, Rahn was fit, trained in survival techniques and an experienced climber. It seemed highly suspicious that he had died just a few weeks after 'resigning' from the SS – the very same month that his colleague, Karl Maria Wiligut, was also forced to resign his commission only to be put under the 'protection' of the Gestapo. Was it possible that Rahn, the occult scholar, and

Wiligut, the certifiable visionary, shared a secret that had put both their lives at risk?

There is the distinct likelihood that Rahn committed ritual suicide by starving himself to death on his beloved mountain in the manner of the 13th-century Gnostic sect, the Cathars, with whom he shared a spiritual bond. It is surely no coincidence that his death occurred on the anniversary of the fall of Montsegur, the aesthetics' mountain stronghold, in southern France, which occurred on 14 March 1244.

Rahn's connection with the Cathars is the key to the mystery, for it also ties in with Himmler's quest for the Holy Grail, the cup which Jesus is said to have used at the Last Supper and which, legend says, caught drops of his blood at the Crucifixion. Himmler believed that the Cathars were custodians of the Grail and that it had been smuggled out of Montsegur before Pope Innocent's forces overwhelmed the fortress and massacred the survivors. While it may seem unlikely that a rabid anti-Christian such as Himmler would search the earth for an iconic Christian symbol, it is upon this central misunderstanding that the whole strange affair revolves.

To Himmler, the Grail could not possibly be a Christian symbol for the simple reason that Jesus was not a Jew but an Aryan. The Nazis held that orthodox Christianity bore no relation to the true teachings of Jesus or the original Christian sect which the disciples had founded.

Nazi doctrine asserted that the Church, meaning the Catholic Church, had appropriated the name and principles of the true

Christians in order to enrich itself at the people's expense. The Nazis justified their avowed intention of replacing Christian services and symbols with their own by arguing that their brand of paganism was not anti-Christian but true Christianity! They saw themselves as rescuing 'true religion', whatever that might mean, from a corrupt Church and returning it to the people. While they may have had cause to criticize the wealth and power of the Church, their Orwellian doublethink did not fool anyone.

PAGAN PROPAGANDA

'Wotan is nearer to us than the Christian God.'
Fr Felix Fischer-Dodeleben (Monastery of Olivia)

Hitler spoke fervently and frequently against organized religion, having denounced the Catholic God as cruel and impotent for failing to intervene when his mother lay dying of cancer.

> *'The religions are all alike, no matter what they call themselves. They have no future – certainly none for the Germans ... Whether it is the Old Testament or the New Testament, it's all the same old Jewish swindle ... One is either a German or a Christian. You cannot be both.'*

It was clear that National Socialism was to be the new religion, or rather a revival of the 'old religion', meaning paganism.

'Our peasants have not forgotten their true religion. It still lives ... The old beliefs will be brought back to honour again ... The peasant will be told what the Church has destroyed for him: the whole secret knowledge of nature, of the divine, the shapeless, the daemonic ... We shall wash off the Christian veneer and bring out a religion peculiar to our race ... our peasantry still lives in heathen beliefs and values ... through the peasantry we shall really be able to destroy Christianity because there is in them a true religion rooted in nature and blood.'

The new symbolism: the Nazis organized art exhibitions and launched them with great pomp. Here, the German eagle is dragged past Hitler by a motley retinue but the effect is more kitsch than classical.

And, if Hermann Rauschning is to be believed, one night in 1933 Hitler announced his intention of tearing up Christianity 'root and branch'. He declared:

> 'We must prevent the churches from doing anything but what they are doing now, that is, losing ground day by day. Do you really believe the masses will ever be Christian again? Nonsense! Never again. That story is finished. No one will listen to it again. But we can hasten matters. The parsons will be made to dig their own graves. They will betray their god to us.'

Rauschning has recently been discredited as a witness to history, but even if his quotations are questionable, another influential Nazi voiced the regime's dislike of organized religion in no uncertain terms. Alfred Rosenberg had written of the day he hoped to establish a National Reich Church:

> 'On the day of its foundation the Christian cross must be removed from all churches, cathedrals and chapels and it must be superseded by the only unconquerable symbol – the swastika.'

Himmler, however, would have preferred to do away with organized religion altogether.

At the funeral of Reinhard Heydrich he said:

> *'This Christendom, this greatest pestilence which could have befallen us in history, which has weakened us with every conflict, we must finish with.'*

A LUCIFEREAN REFORMATION

Incredibly Hitler's enthusiasm for a root-and-branch reformation of Christianity was shared by those who should have known better – the academics and the intelligentsia.

Professor Ernst Bergmann of Leipzig University, an art critic with theological pretensions, set out the Nazi justification for the deification of the Führer in *Die 25 Thesen der Deutschreligion* ('The Twenty-five Articles of Faith of the German Religion').

'Away with Rome and Jerusalem!' he spat, referring to the Catholic Church and Judaism. 'Back to our native German Faith. Our religion is no more that of the international Christ-God who could not stop Versailles.' Christianity, according to Professor Bergmann, was 'an unnatural religion ... the creation of a pre-eminently Oriental mind ... which contradicts at almost every point the German sense of custom and morality.'

The new German religion would worship Wotan, the god of knowledge, and the congregation would accept Adolf Hitler as their messiah.

> *'Everyone who seeks a pure religion and a pure life of God must keep himself painfully remote from the Bible and*

> *Christianity. For there is a Satan in this religion ... We are*
> *no longer the ancient Germans. That does not prevent us*
> *from entering deeply into the German forest-religion and*
> *from realizing that the Gothic dome is an imitation in stone*
> *of the Germanic holy forest-place and that Gothic in its*
> *entirety derives from the German soul ... Mankind indeed*
> *requires urgently to be free of Christianity and the Saviour*
> *"from beyond"...We will no longer believe in Christ. We*
> *will be Christ ourselves and act as a Christ.'*

THE SEARCH FOR THE GRAIL

Which brings us back to the Grail and Himmler's adoption of it
as a priceless Aryan relic. Although it is commonly believed that
the Grail is an artefact of Christian origin, the 'cup of light' is a
symbol of the Higher Self in the Western esoteric tradition and
may well be yet another 'pagan' idea shamelessly purloined by
the early Church. It seems more likely that Himmler envisaged
the Grail in the form described by Wolfram von Eschenbach in
Parzival which was that of a sacred stone, the *lapis exilis* of the
alchemists. Possibly he didn't care what form it took so long as
it was a vessel of occult power through which he could channel
the cosmic forces that would ensure the invincibility of the SS.

Otto Rahn, a devotee of von Eschenbach and Wagner, was
convinced that the object of his lifelong obsession was a sacred
stone and he travelled throughout Europe during 1931 in search

of proof. He claimed to have found it in a small French town called Ussat-les-Bains in the Languedoc region under the guidance of a fellow enthusiast Antonin Gadal. Gadal was a member of a historical society known as the 'Friends of Montsegur and the Grail' and he had stocked a small private museum with artefacts and documents from the period which Rahn found invaluable.

After transcribing the ancient documents and deciphering the inscriptions on the relics provided by Gadal, Rahn concluded that Montsavat, the legendary mountain of the Grail, was in reality the Cathar stronghold, Montsegur.

Having decoded the sacred geometry of the site and its relationship to other sites, he became convinced that the Cathar treasure would not have been removed from such a holy place but must have been hidden in a secret location known only to the elders, most likely underground where it would have remained unharmed when the pope's knights set the fortress aflame.

The result of his researches was published in 1933 under the title *Kreuzzug gegen den Graal* (Crusade Against the Grail) which concluded that Parsifal, the Grail Knight, had been a Cathar. Inevitably, the book came to the attention of Reichsführer SS Himmler.

HIMMLER'S RASPUTIN

It is said that Rahn only agreed to accept a commission in the SS because it guaranteed him a square meal three times a day and unlimited funds to pursue his research. Whatever the reason, he certainly lived to regret it as it put him under intolerable pressure to produce results and it introduced him to the eccentric and unpredictable Karl Maria Wiligut.

Wiligut, who had designed the Death's Head ring for the SS and was commonly referred to as 'Himmler's Rasputin', had at one time been certified insane which made him the ideal Nazi expert on the occult. Himmler was suitably impressed with the wild-eyed rune scholar and clairvoyant to the extent that he had bestowed on him the title of Head of the Department of Prehistory at the SS Race and Resettlement Office. Wiligut's qualifications for this prestigious post were his knowledge of runes and his ability to access 20,000 years of Teutonic history from the Akashic Records, the collective memory of every human being or, as Jung termed it, the Collective Unconscious. From this cloud of all-knowing energy, he learned that Christianity was of German origin and that Jesus was in fact the Teutonic god Baldur who had fled to the Middle East after surviving an attempt to crucify him by devotees of his rival, Wotan. Quite what Rahn, a conventional historian, thought of his new colleague is not known, but he must have wondered what madhouse he had stumbled into.

Whatever misgivings Rahn had, he kept them to himself. His correspondence with Wiligut concerning his quest for the Grail, which took him as far afield as Iceland, was restricted to dry academic reports on the symbolic significance of ancient place names. When he returned, Himmler made his displeasure known and gave Rahn until 31 October 1936, to provide a publishable manuscript documenting proof of Aryan superiority and Germany's right to the lands to the east, specifically Russia. Or better still, evidence that there were underground passages at Montsegur containing the Grail and possibly other occult artefacts, as Rahn had originally suspected. In *Hitler and the Cathar Tradition*, French author Jean-Michel Angebert speculates that Rahn succeeded in locating the passages and recovering the Grail with the help of an SS *Ahnenerbe* archaeological team. The Holy Cup was then crated up and transported under guard to Wewelsburg where it was placed on a marble pedestal in the Realm of the Dead underneath the Great Hall.

This seems highly improbable for several reasons, the main one being that mystics believe the Grail to be purely symbolic of the heightened level of awareness known as the Christ Consciousness which can only be attained through a spiritual quest. This accounts for its enduring fascination for spiritual seekers of all traditions – not only Christian mystics. Besides, artefacts – be they tarot cards, crystal balls, runes or even the celebrated Spear of Destiny – have no inherent power of their own; the power comes from those who use the object to stimulate their own psychic sensitivities. Rahn duly produced his report, 'Lucifer's Court', whose title and central theme betrayed the extent to which he had fallen under Himmler's spell. A typical passage reads as follows:

> *'... the ancient god of love is also the lord of Spring as personified in the Greek myth of Apollo, who brought back the light from the sun, he is a light-bearer, or "Lucifer". According to the Apocalypse of John, Apollo*

> *was identified with the Devil ... There is much more [light*
> *in the world] than in the houses of God – cathedrals and*
> *churches – where Lucifer is neither able nor desirous of*
> *entering because of the sombre stained-glass windows on*
> *which the Jewish prophets and apostles, the Roman (i.e.*
> *Catholic) gods and saints are depicted.'*

In essence, Rahn is attempting to legitimize the Nazis' rejection of orthodox Christianity by claiming that the early Church demonized the true god, Lucifer, who is not to be confused with the devil, or Satan. Satan was Jehovah, the false God of the Jews, which proves that Jesus could not possibly have been a Jew and that all Jews are in reality Satanists!

Even the lunatic Wiligut could not have invented a more twisted theory, but Rahn appears to have been sincere in his beliefs. A newspaper report of a lecture he gave on the subject at the Dietrich Eckart House in Dortmund in January 1938 revealed his continuing loyalty to the Cathars. Speaking of the fall of Montsegur, he said:

> *'205 leading followers of Lucifer were burnt on a huge pyre*
> *by Dominicans in the South of France after a large-scale*
> *priestly Crusade in the name of Christian clemency. With*
> *fire and sword the Lucifer doctrine of the Light-Bearer*
> *was persecuted along with its followers. The [Cathars] are*
> *dead, but their spirit lives on.'*

Rahn was as much a victim of Nazism, one might argue, as any of the innumerable innocents who were murdered by them. But Rahn lost not only his life, he lost his soul.

THE OCCULT BUREAU

It is fitting that the man appointed by Himmler to head the Nazi occult bureau should bear such a striking resemblance to the traditional image of Mephistopheles, for if any branch of the Nazi administration had been conceived in hell it was this one. Its official name was the *Ahnenerbe*, or Department of Ancestral Heritage, an innocuous title masking some of the most perverse activities ever conceived by the human mind, including sadistic experiments on concentration camp inmates. The bureau's senior administrator, SS Colonel Wolfram Sievers, cultivated a trim black beard and a veneer of urbane charm giving him the appearance of the devil himself, and there is reason to suspect that, when he walked calmly to the gallows at Nuremberg prison in 1948, he did so in the belief that his infernal master awaited him.

Prior to its assimilation into the SS in 1935, the *Ahnenerbe* had been a pseudo-scientific institution staffed by academics studying the nutritional value of various forms of honey, the occult symbolism of the Etonian top hat and the mystical significance of the suppression of the Celtic harp in Northern Ireland! Such trivial pursuits had been presided over by Sievers' predecessor, Herman Wirth, a man whose sanity was as questionable as that of Wiligut.

At the entrance to his home, Wirth had pinned a notice which read: 'No smoking. A deep breather lives here.' It referred to his wife, a medium, who remained in a permanent trance-like state, while her husband stood by in expectation ready to record the profound cosmic truths he claimed she was able to channel from higher intelligences. Wirth had secured the post of head of the *Ahnenerbe* after impressing Himmler with his knowledge of prehistory, but he was gullible in the extreme and embraced every crackpot theory at face value. He trusted his intuition to inform him whether a questionable source was genuine or not, rather than demanding documentary evidence or scientific proof. His unshakeable belief in the mythical German homeland of Thule, for example, was based entirely on 'evidence' offered by the patently fake *Uralinda Chronicle*, a supposed Nordic document which bore a 19th-century watermark. When its authenticity was questioned, he justified his faith in it by saying that it was a copy and that he trusted that the original would surface when the owner felt the time was right.

Himmler was forced to defend Wirth's reputation on more than one occasion, if only to save his own. In 1933, he ordered Hermann Rauschning to strong-arm dissenting academics into silence, so that Wirth's assertions would go unchallenged.

'Himmler called me to account about a professor who lectured on prehistoric times both at Danzig and at Königsberg. This man, he said, had been criticising current ideas about the origin of the Teutons and the age

A 1938 portrait of Hitler by Hubert Lanzinger entitled 'The Standard Bearer'; it depicts Hitler as an archetypcal Teutonic knight and saviour of Germany.

of their civilisation, and had condemned these ideas from allegedly scientific points of view. At that time a sensation had been created by an exceedingly silly book, a manifest forgery, the Uralinda Chronicle. *The book traced back the history of the Teutons to an infinitely remote period: and it proved once more that the original German-Teuton race was the true creator of European civilisation. The professor had treated this book with proper severity [i.e. criticism], and Himmler wanted me to dispose once and for all of this type of scientific mischief-making. He himself would put the fear of God into the professors of Königsberg and Breslau: I was to do the same in Danzig ... I heard a lecture by the professor who had edited the peculiar "Chronicle", Professor Wirth; he had written some queer books on the "Origin of Humanity", and had engaged in research into the primitive symbolism of prehistoric ages in signs and designs. Hitler was interested in the subject. Wirth spoke at meetings in which the fundamentals of a new conception of God and the basis of the coming civilization were discussed ... Humanity, we learned, stood on the threshold of a new day. Every principle accepted at the present day was far gone in obsolescence. Nothing could be of any service to us in the new era now dawning, but recollections and resuscitations of the earliest ideas and customs of the dawn of humanity ... Prehistory is the doctrine of the eminence of the Germans at the dawn of civilization.'*

However, Himmler eventually tired of having to defend Wirth's unsubstantiated claims and replaced him with the staunchly loyal Wolfram Sievers. From the day he took office, Sievers implemented a root-and-branch restructuring of the entire institute, expanding it to 50 separate departments, including the notorious 'Military Experimental Science' unit, which instigated human refrigeration experiments at Dachau Concentration Camp.

It has been fashionable for some individuals with a limited understanding of the regime to regard the Nazis as buffoons and certainly some of their more bizarre theories regarding lost subterranean cities, Aryan ancestry and the Hollow Earth are laughable. But it needs to be remembered that their ignorance and inhumanity had horrific consequences for those who were subjected to intolerable suffering in pursuit of the new 'science'.

A Dachau prisoner, who was forced to assist in tests to determine the effects of high altitude for the Luftwaffe, later described the effects of decompression suffered by prisoners.

> '[They] would go mad and pull out their hair in an effort to relieve the pressure. They would tear their hair and face with their fingers and nails in an effort to maim themselves in their madness. They would beat the wall with their hands and head and scream in an attempt to relieve the pressure on their ear drums …'

When the Luftwaffe complained that the tests had failed to take account of the effects of sub-zero temperatures at high altitude and on pilots who might have to bale out over the Arctic Ocean, the MES (mine protection command) obliged by ordering that malnourished prisoners should be left out all night and buckets of freezing water thrown over them at regular intervals. As Francis King pointed out in *Satan and Swastika* (1976), the only decent human beings involved in these 'disgustingly cruel and scientifically valueless' experiments were the victims. He cites one particular episode reported to him as an example by a camp inmate in which two Russian officers were brought in and forced completely naked into a tank of freezing water.

> *'Hour after hour passed, though cold narcosis usually occurs in sixty minutes. In this case the two were still fully conscious at the end of two and one half hours. All efforts on our part to persuade [the camp doctor] to give them a narcotic injection were in vain. Sometime during the third hour one of the Russians said to the other: "Comrade, ask the officer to shoot us." The other replied that he didn't expect any mercy from that Fascist dog. Then they shook hands with a "Farewell, Comrade!" ... The experiment lasted at least five hours before death finally occurred.'*

The senior physician in charge of the Dachau tests was Dr Sigmund Rascher. He escaped Allied justice but was shot by SS guards on Himmler's orders in the last weeks of the war. The Reichsführer had endorsed Rascher's sadistic treatment of unarmed prisoners, but had drawn the line at being lied to by the physician who had accepted a gift from Himmler for having fathered three children in late middle age. In fact, Rascher and his wife had kidnapped three babies from an orphanage and claimed them as their own.

It is estimated that the *Ahnenerbe* spent more on their 'researches' than the Americans invested in developing the first atom bomb.

RUNES

If there was one arcane obsession shared by both the *völkisch* occultists and the Nazis other than race, it was the runes which featured on the helmets, weapons, banners and armoured vehicles of the German army for reasons largely unknown to their enemies – until after the war.

According to Norse legend, the Runic 'alphabet' was given to mankind by Odin, the one-eyed god who wanders the world of men dispensing wisdom and justice. In the 13th-century Icelandic legend, the Volsunga Saga, Brynhyld (Brunhilde) instructs Sigund (Siegfried) that runes are the 'root of all things' and assures him that if he carved the Tyr rune on his sword hilt it would ensure victory in battle – a practice adopted 600 years later by the SS. The association with magic derives from the fact that runes predate the written word in Europe – their stark, simple outlines being carved in stone, metal and wood which imprinted the material with the residual personal energy of the scribe.

Runes were widely used throughout Europe from 400 BC to protect the sacred burial places of the dead and in the casting of spells and curses. Written language replaced them at the end of the Middle Ages, but even today they retain their occult associations. Runes are still used for divination, or the magician can meditate on a specific symbol to awaken the corresponding quality or attribute in themselves.

It is an ideographic 'alphabet' similar to Egyptian hieroglyphs and Chinese characters: each rune stands for more than a letter, it is a symbol, representing a significant word or concept. Each is said to possess the essence of that idea which can be accessed by an initiate of rune magic who seeks to tap into its primal force. For this reason the *völkisch* occultists argued that runes were the true expression of ancient Aryan culture, whereas written script was Semitic and superficial.

The origin and meaning of the runes were an obsession of the Aryan academics of the *Ahnenerbe* who greeted each discovery of runic script in a distant land as validation of German territorial claims, the inference being that the country in question must have been settled by the Teutonic peoples in ancient times. One eminent Runic scholar, Josef Heinsch, went so far as to suggest that leylines running through the Rhineland actually formed huge runic characters which accounted for the mystical significance of the region.

Meanwhile, the mystical significance of the runes inspired Himmler to adopt those which he believed would act as talismans to protect or inspire his men. The double *sig* rune used by the

SS for example, represents victory and therefore, by adopting it as their insignia, those who wore it would invoke everything associated with successful conquest, including courage, strength, unity, duty and physical energy. Himmler's intense interest in the magical power of the runes led him to make it compulsory for SS officers to attend courses in runic lore.

 The *Hakenkreuz* (hooked cross) was the pagan symbol for Thor, the God of Thunder.

 The *Sonnenrad* (or Sunwheel) swastika was the ancient Norse symbol of the Sun. It was adopted by the 5th SS Panzer Division, *Wiking*.

 The *Sig-Rune* represented victory. Contrary to popular myth, it had a mundane origin, having been designed in 1932 by an employee of Ferdinand Hoffstatter, badge-makers.

 The *Ger-Rune* was a symbol of community spirit and of 'belonging'.

 The *Wolfsangel* (or Wolf Hook) was said to ward off danger. It was adopted by the 2nd SS Panzer Division, Das Reich. A variation on the *Wolfsangel* was the insignia of the Dutch SS.

The *Opfer-Rune* represented self-sacrifice and was used to commemorate the Nazis who were killed in the Munich Putsch of 1923.

The *Eif-Rune* symbolized devotion and loyalty. It was worn by Hitler's personal adjutants.

The *Leben-Rune* (or Life Rune) was the symbol of the *Lebensborn* Society which cared for the illegitimate children of SS men.

The *Toten-Rune* symbolized death and can be seen on Waffen-SS graves.

The *Tyr-Rune* (or Battle Rune) was the ancient symbol of Tyr, the god of war.

The *Heilszeichen* represented prosperity and appeared on the *SS Totenkopfring* (or Death's Head Ring) awarded to SS officers.

The *Hagal-Rune* (*hagal* means 'hail') symbolizes faith.

The *Odal-Rune* represented friendship and kinship through blood. It was adopted by the SS Race and Settlement Office and by the 7th SS *Freiwilligen Gebirgs* Division, *Prinz Eugen*.

Chapter Six

THE SS: MYTH OF THE 'BLACK KNIGHTS'

'The vital idea that inspired the SA was replaced ...
by an idea that was purely Satanic, the SS.'

Joachim Gunthe (1934)

There was nothing noble or chivalrous about the SS (*Schutzstaffel* or Personal Guard) whose name became synonymous with brutality and mass murder. They were collectively responsible for the death of 14 million innocent civilians and the destruction of innumerable communities and cultures throughout Europe. As overseers of the concentration and death camps, they were directly responsible for the murder of 6 million Jews, as well as 5 million Russians, 2 million Poles, 500,000 gypsies and a further 500,000 of their own countrymen whom they murdered because they were homosexual, disabled or opposed to the Nazi regime.

In their own minds and in the fantasies of their leader, former chicken farmer Heinrich Himmler, the SS were the embodiment of the chivalric spirit and the reincarnation of the Teutonic knights who were entrusted with the preservation of the Aryan ideal and the extermination of the 'inferior races', namely the Jews and Slavs. In a cynical attempt to establish continuity with Prussian military tradition, Himmler had named his new SS regiments after those which had brought glory to the Empire in the days of the Kaiser and the campaigns against Napoleon. But the men of the *Totenkopf*, *Liebstandarte* and *Das Reich* brought only dishonour to their fatherland. Originally formed in 1922 as an elite personal bodyguard for the Führer, there were still fewer than 200 men when Himmler was appointed Reichsführer in 1929 at the age of 28. Within four years, his organizational skills had multiplied their ranks to approximately 50,000. By 1934, the year after Hitler's accession to power, their numbers had grown to such an extent that Himmler could afford to expel 60,000 'undesirables' in a bloodless purge. But it was only after the 'Night of the Long Knives' on 30 June 1934, when SS execution squads rounded up and butchered the SA leadership, including its figurehead Ernst Röhm, that the supreme authority of the Black Order was assured. From that day on, the brown-shirted street brawlers of the SA, as well as the Security Service (SD) and even the dreaded Gestapo, the Nazi Secret Police, were subordinate to the SS.

Himmler had remarked with grim satisfaction: 'I know that there are many in Germany who feel sick when they see this black tunic, we can understand that.' And he was unapologetic when it came to justifying his men's ruthless methods.

'One principle must be absolute for the SS man: we must be honest, decent, loyal and comradely to members of our own blood and to no one else. What happens to the Russians, what happens to the Czechs, is a matter of utter indifference to me. Such good blood of our own kind as there may be among the nations we shall acquire for ourselves, if necessary by taking away the children and bringing them up among us. Whether the other peoples live in comfort or perish of hunger interests me only in so far as we need them as slaves for our culture, apart from that it does not interest me. Whether or not 10,000 Russian women collapse from exhaustion while digging a tank ditch interests me only in so far as the tank ditch is completed for Germany.'

BLOOD AND SOIL

Ironically, Himmler, the slight, unassuming son of a Catholic schoolteacher who rose from pedantic petty party bureaucrat to command one of the most feared fighting units in history, was said to turn pale at the sight of blood. His sadistic streak had to be satisfied vicariously by others who willingly dirtied their hands on his behalf.

As with many in the Nazi hierarchy, he considered himself a man of culture, principles and ideals. He had studied agriculture at the University of Munich and dreamed of establishing an agricultural academy which would lead a rural revival. 'The yeoman on his own acre is the backbone of the German people's strength and character,' he had written. If Himmler had prevailed, German industry would have been dismantled and the nation would have been forcibly regressed to the Middle Ages, centred around a feudalistic self-sufficient peasant economy with himself as liege and lord.

According to his adjutants, the Reichsführer envisioned himself as the reincarnation of King Heinrich der Vogler (Henry the Fowler AD875–936), King of Saxony and founder of the First Reich whom he described as 'the noble peasant of his people'. It is unclear if he took this idea literally as, according to his personal physician Felix Kersten, he was also in the habit of conversing aloud with the spirit of his hero in the dead of night. This apparent contradiction is explained by the fact that Himmler subscribed to the theory put forward by the mystic

Karl Eckhart, who believed that each individual is part of a soul group and so is drawn to reincarnate within the group.

According to this theory, a man might return as his own grandson, or a father and son might be reborn a century later as brothers in order to resolve the differences that divided them in their previous lifetime. Himmler was not ashamed to express his belief in such unconventional and anti-Christian ideas in public. In Dachau, on the thousandth anniversary of Henry the Fowler's death in 1936, he told an audience of high-ranking SS officers that they were part of an esoteric order who had known each other in a previous lifetime and had been brought together again to fulfil a special mission after which they could expect to meet again in a future life. The following year he ordered 20,000 copies of Eckhart's book, *Temporal Immortality*, to be distributed among SS members, but the order was cancelled after several of Hitler's inner circle convinced the Führer that Himmler's advocacy of Eastern esotericism was undermining the regime's relationship with the Church.

Such was Himmler's devotion to his namesake, Heinrich, that he made an annual pilgrimage to his tomb to renew his vow to continue the king's 'civilising mission in the East' and sat beside it in silent meditation in the hope of receiving guidance and inspiration from the dead monarch.

Ancestry, heritage, culture and the sacred nature of the land loomed large in Himmler's mythos, giving rise to the pernicious Nazi revision of the Blood and Soil doctrine, which maintained that the Aryans were *Übermenschen*, the Master Race, to be serviced by slaves like the Pharaohs of ancient Egypt. Clearly, his concept of German peasant life was not the pastoral idyll of the German romantic poets. He envisaged the fields of the Fatherland being tilled by Slavic slave labourers, including children, who would toil from dusk to dawn until they dropped dead from starvation and overwork, while their German masters looked on unmoved. Tragically, his vision became reality for hundreds of thousands of human beings.

SS INITIATION

With his unimposing physique, poor eyesight and chronic digestive disorders, Himmler made a pathetic figurehead for his Praetorian Guard. Nevertheless, entry requirements for the SS were initially stringent in the extreme – although they were later relaxed to accommodate suitable candidates in the occupied countries, especially after the defeat at Stalingrad when the ranks of the SS were severely depleted.

In addition to qualifying as exceptional physical specimens of Nordic manhood, officers had to prove their Aryan ancestry back to 1750, while lower ranks only had to demonstrate that their family tree was untainted by Jewish blood as far back as 1900. Exceptions were made for Himmler's favourites who were suspected of having Jewish ancestors, such as 'iron-hearted' Reinhard Heydrich of whom Himmler said, 'He had overcome the Jew in himself by intellectual means.' The whole Nazi

Heinrich Himmler (1900–1945), supreme leader of the SS, ensured that all his troops learned 'how to kill and how to die'.

concept of a pure Aryan race was as farcical as it was tragic, for even Himmler had to admit to having Jewish relatives by marriage.

Once accepted, the typical 18-year-old SS novice underwent a lengthy period of training and indoctrination during which he was permitted to wear the uniform but without the collar patches. These were awarded on 9 November each year, on the first anniversary of the 1923 putsch which followed his acceptance into the order.

On the following 30 January, the anniversary of Hitler's accession to power, the candidate would receive his provisional SS identity card, but he had to wait until 20 April, Hitler's birthday, before being given a full identity card and the collar patches.

In addition to his military training which was designed, in Himmler's words, to teach every man 'how to kill and how to die', candidates were subjected to indoctrination in the SS credo, a perversion of the Catholic catechism which demanded that every man memorize the answers to such leading questions as: 'Why do we believe in Germany and the Führer?' (The required answer ran as follows: 'Because we believe in God, we believe in Germany which He created in His world and in the Führer, Adolf Hitler, whom He has sent us.') Once the credo was learnt, the candidate was required to attend a neo-pagan initiation ceremony which culminated with him taking an oath that was intended to bind his fate to that of his Führer even unto death.

> *'I swear to thee Adolf Hitler ... loyalty and bravery.*
> *'I swear to thee and the superiors thou shalt appoint*
> *obedience unto death. So help me God.'*

It was by exploiting the German trait of unquestioning obedience to authority in this way that the Nazis ensnared so many innocent young men into blind obedience to their vile orders.

Obedience was equated with religious observance and authority with the Divine Will. To question the State and its figurehead was tantamount to questioning the Will of God.

It has long been thought that such oaths were initiated by the Nazis, but in fact they had previously been implemented by Kaiser Wilhelm II. On 10 December 1891, he had told recruits:

> *'You have now sworn allegiance to me in the presence*
> *of a priest of God and before this altar. You have sworn*
> *allegiance to me. This means you are now my soldiers. You*
> *have given yourselves to me body and soul. You know*
> *henceforth only one enemy, my enemy ... I may order you*
> *to shoot down your own relatives, your brothers or even*
> *your parents – which certainly God forbid! – but even then*
> *you must obey my orders without question.'*

Only after his obligatory service in the Labour Corps and the Army was the successful candidate entitled to wear full SS insignia and carry a ceremonial dagger engraved with runic symbols which were intended to bestow magical powers of protection on the wearer. The SS insignia were not, as many have thought, representative of lightning flashes but were two *sig* runes which were symbolic of power and victory.

Since ancient times, the dagger has been considered a sacred weapon and was used in ceremonial magic where it represented the grounding of the god force in the realm of matter, in the same way that a lightning rod channels electricity to the earth.

Prior to 1939, all ranks also received a silver death's head signet ring, but during the war it was given only to SS commanders who had held a senior rank for more than three years. Again, the ring was a clear counterpart to the magical rings worn by the pagan priests of ancient times. In Germany these were known as the *gothi*.

After serving in the Labour Corps or the Army, the SS novice was assigned to whichever branch of the service his superiors deemed most suitable for his particular skills.

The SS had their own regular army unit, the Waffen SS, who were considered Hitler's loyal shock troops; in the concentration camps, the SS doubled as guards and executioners, or they could be transferred to duties supervising and assisting the Gestapo to round up and interrogate members of the resistance in occupied countries.

The most notorious unit of all was the *Einsatzgruppe*, or death squad, whose sole duty was to act as an extermination unit, instigating Hitler's policy of 'ethnic cleansing', or genocide, in the wake of the advancing German troops.

FROM CRADLE TO GRAVE

Every aspect of the SS man's life, from his baptism to his funeral, was controlled by the state. At baptism, the first-born would receive a personal gift from the Reichsführer in the form of a silver-plated mug, while the fourth child received a silver candlestick engraved with the legend, 'You are but a link in the endless chain of the [SS] clan.' Himmler even issued instructions on how his men should commit suicide 'in the proper fashion', so as not to bring dishonour to the regiment. Even in death the SS were distinguished from the regular troops by a wooden *Toten* rune in place of the conventional cross on their graves.

A dossier was kept on each member detailing every aspect of their public and private lives, including their financial affairs. Even their prospective marriage partners were screened to ensure 'the conditions of race and healthy stock were fulfilled'. Once they had been approved, even the ceremony was Nazified, purged of Christian elements and officiated over by the local SS leader who replaced the priest. On 3 May 1943, Himmler made his views on conventional Christian marriage explicit.

'Marriage as it is today is the Satanic work of the Roman Catholic Church. Regarded dispassionately and without prejudice, our present marriage laws are absolutely immoral ... [they] lead to a decrease in the size of families. After the war ... monogamy will cease to be enforced upon promiscuous mankind. The SS and the heroes of this war

will have special privileges. They will immediately have the right to take a second wife, who shall be considered to be as legitimate as the first. The permission to have two wives will be a mark of distinction ... The racially pure blood of German heroes will be transmitted to as many offspring as possible ... Any soldier who has distinguished himself in the war ... will be allowed to replace a non-Aryan wife with one who is pure Aryan.'

Himmler's obsessive interest in the procreation of healthy Aryan offspring is said to have found its ultimate expression in the *Lebensborn*, SS stud farms to which every unmarried woman over thirty was required to report and to 'put herself at their disposal to be made pregnant'.

Ironically, these human breeding farms proved inexplicably unproductive. The infant mortality rate was twice the national average despite the administration of calming herbal teas whose ingredients were cultivated in gardens attached to the concentration camps.

GHOSTS AND GRAVEYARDS

It is no exaggeration to say that the Nazis had some very odd ideas indeed. Considering that their leaders were no more than street thugs and petty bureaucrats, it is unsurprising that they embraced such eccentric theories as Bender's 'Hollow Earth' model or Hörbiger's 'World Ice Theory'.

The perfect Nazi wedding: Magda Goebbels once claimed she married Joseph in 1931 to be closer to the Führer, who can be seen behind young Harald Quandt, the son from her previous marriage.

But perhaps the most bizarre practice was that advocated by the SS newspaper *Die Schwarze Korps* (The Black Corps), which encouraged its readers to copulate in graveyards where German heroes had been interred.

Lists of suitable sites were published only after they had been approved by the *Ahnenerbe* department of the SS whose job it was to ensure that the cemeteries had not been 'polluted' by non-Aryan spirits. [Source: Nigel Pennick, *Hitler's Secret Sciences*, Neville Spearman, 1981, p.155] Jewish cemeteries were systematically desecrated and the sites redeveloped, but there was one significant exception.

The ancient Jewish cemetery at Worms was spared because the superstitious Himmler believed that the magical geomancy of the site, which dated back to the 11th century would be disturbed if the alignments were altered. It is likely he also feared some form of divine retribution if any of the 2,000 graves were disturbed as the bodies had been buried in sacred sand brought from Jerusalem.

WEWELSBURG CASTLE

'[The castle] *was adapted to serve as a sort of SS monastery. There a secret chapter of the Order assembled each year ... each had to devote himself to a ritual of spiritual exercises aimed mainly at concentration, the equivalent of prayer, before discussing the higher policy of the SS.'*

SS Brigadeführer Walter Schellenberg

When Himmler surveyed the ruins of Schloss Wewelsburg, near Paderborn in Westphalia, in the summer of 1934, he knew immediately that he had found his Camelot. Although it would require several million Reichsmarks to restore it to its former glory – and considerably more to furnish it in a manner befitting the spiritual centre of the SS – there was no doubt in the frugal Himmler's mind that it would be money well spent. Legend had it that the castle would be the last surviving stronghold against a furious future assault by hordes from the East, and

Schloss Wewelsburg was a Nazi Camelot and the 'spiritual centre' of the SS. It was hoped that future generations would visit here on pilgrimages to venerate the founders of the 1,000-year Reich.

the ever-superstitious Himmler intended to be safe behind its impregnable walls. Furthermore, according to occult experts in the *Ahnenerbe*, the fortress was situated at the intersection of several leylines, which meant that the Earth's energies were concentrated at its triangular-shaped foundations and could be evoked during magical rituals to be directed to whatever end the practitioner desired.

Once the local authority had been persuaded to lease Wewelsburg for the nominal rent of one mark per year and the project had secured a government grant, the renovation work began in earnest. Each suite was furnished in a style befitting a German hero and was replete with richly embroidered tapestries, heavy brocade curtains, ornate antique furniture carved from solid oak by the finest craftsmen and plush carpets that would not be out of place in a sultan's palace. Even the wrought-iron door handles and candlesticks were the finest examples of German craftsmanship.

At its heart was the banqueting hall measuring 45 x 30 metres (147 x 98 feet), with its imposing Arthurian round table around which were ranged 13 carved wooden chairs upholstered in pigskin and bearing the name of the Obergruppenführer who was to be honoured with a place at Himmler's court. The number of guests symbolized the 12 signs of the zodiac, with Himmler at its head, but may also have been intended to parody Jesus and the 12 Christian disciples whose influence was to be eradicated with the establishment of the New World Order.

Directly below the Great Hall lay the hushed stone circular

vault known as 'the realm of the dead' which housed 12 black pedestals, each in a niche ranged around a hollow shaft. This was the crypt in which the fallen 'knights' were to find their eternal rest. In the event that their bodies could not be recovered from the battlefield, their coats-of-arms were to be burnt in their stead and the ashes placed in a porcelain urn. Here, it was hoped, future generations would venerate the founders of the 1,000-year Reich.

The official line was that Wewelsburg was to serve as an SS training school, but at least one insider witnessed magical rites being performed in an antechamber of the castle.

In his memoirs, SS Brigadeführer Walter Schellenberg recalls the moment he inadvertently walked in on a psychic circle whose members had been instructed to project their mental energy into an adjacent room where a suspect (General Von Fritsch) was being questioned.

> '[Himmler had] *ordered them all to concentrate their minds on exerting a suggestive influence over the General that would induce him to tell the truth ... to see these twelve SS leaders sitting in a circle, all sunk in deep and silent contemplation, was indeed a remarkable sight.*'

With his distinctive rituals, oaths and insignia every SS man was made to understand that he was more than merely a member of an elite fighting unit. He was an initiate in a secret religious order, a superior being in an amoral universe existing beyond the human concepts of Good and Evil.

The SS leadership with Himmler second from the left, and Reinhard Heydrich second from the right... they counted themselves as belonging to a long line of German knights.

In practical terms, he was above the law, no court had jurisdiction over the SS.

Only his superiors could judge him. He was conditioned to act without compassion for his enemies and without mercy for those condemned by the state as unworthy of life, for they were *Untermenschen* (subhumans). Once he put on the black uniform, he was not required to have a conscience or a thought of his own. He could kill with impunity and consider every brutal act a service to the state.

Chapter Seven

SATAN AND THE SWASTIKA

'If something profoundly evil does not lurk behind Germany's present tyranny, where, indeed, is evil to be found?'

Lewis Spence, 'Occult Causes of the Present War' (1940)

In 1940, the British occult historian Lewis Spence, author of a bestselling book on Atlantis, published an anti-Nazi pamphlet ('Occult Causes of the Present War') in which he voiced what many people had suspected for years – the idea that Nazi Germany was the creation of satanic forces intent on instigating a new Dark Age. 'In this work,' Spence declared, 'the author reveals the nature and existence of hidden powers at work behind the Nazi organization, which he believes is but the outward, though appropriate, manifestation of satanist and diabolic agencies which employ it for their own malignant purposes.' Spence was not, as one might imagine, in the employ of Allied 'black propaganda' agencies, but was genuinely convinced that socio-economic factors, militant nationalism and the power of Hitler's personality alone could not account for the emergence of this new evil empire.

> '... the Führer is merely the creature and instrument of forces which for centuries have been making use of this or that dictator, tyrant or other puppet notoriety to further their own arcane intentions, which, in a word, are the creation of general chaos and the final destruction of humanity.'

Spence argued that practically every European revolution was instigated by those who sought to overthrow Christianity and therefore there must have been a malevolent intelligence exercising its influence on the disaffected, ruthlessly ambitious and impressionable in Germany between the wars, as there had been in revolutionary Russia, in Robespierre's France and in Franco's Spain, although Franco's 'conservative revolution' had been actively supported by the Catholic Church.

> *'... the new pagan movement in Germany, the uncompromisingly Satanic origin of its method and intention admits of but little dispute. The replacement of the Cross by the swastika, the abrogation of the Sacrament in favour of a rite resembling that of the mysteries of Demeter, the persecution of the Christian churches and of their priests and ministers, and the replacement of the ritual, or service and hymnology by blasphemous offices and songs, the erection of a new godhead, the instruction of the young in the myths of the past instead of in the Scriptures – all this affords the clearest proof of Germany's relapse into that type of paganism which the Satanist policy and propaganda have invariably regarded as the most fitting medium for the destruction and extirpation of the Christian faith.'*

Of course, being a vociferous opponent of Christianity or organized religion per se, does not necessarily qualify someone as a Satanist. That was the spurious argument of the early Church. More often those seeking to loosen the stranglehold of the Church, and particularly the Catholic Church, were simply aspiring to self-determination or social reform.

But Spence, and other writers who shared his belief in Good and Evil, pointed to the deep-rooted practice of witchcraft and magic in Germany, which they presented as prima facie evidence that the country was a breeding ground for the black arts, while the Germans' morbid fascination with the dark lore of the forests proved that the population, specifically the peasantry, were predisposed to paganism. In truth, it was the rural Germans who were the most loyal churchgoers, superstition and ignorance being more likely to drive such people into the paternal protection of the Church than into a coven! But Spence was right in one respect. The German psyche could be said to be inclined to morbid romanticism and the Nazis had conditioned the population to see themselves and their enemies in terms of Wagnerian archetypes. Propaganda portrayed the statuesque blue-eyed, blond men of the SS as Siegfried personified, while the Jews and Slavs were the grasping dwarves of the underworld. Mistrust of the outsider was deeply rooted in the nation's psyche and clearly ripe for exploitation.

This inherent tendency to think in terms of racial stereotypes was not exclusively a German vice, it was symptomatic of this period, as society was reduced to the law of the jungle by the Great Depression. America had its gangsters, Europe had its fascist thugs. Lawlessness and extremism were on the rise across the Western world. Evil, in all its forms was fighting for a foothold in the 20th century. Even the elderly Kaiser was reported to be looking to blame Germany's defeat in the First World War on malign and faceless forces, namely the Freemasons

Nazi propaganda portrayed the blue-eyed Aryan as the ideal. From the age of six, boys were required to live up to this stereotype in the Hitler Youth as they trained for battles to come.

and the mythical (and fictional) occult brotherhood known as the Illuminati, who were reputedly behind every conspiracy in history and continue to be cited in the present day as the unseen hand behind every tragedy from the invasion of Iraq to the 'assassination' of Diana, Princess of Wales!

In his country retreat at Doorn, Kaiser Wilhelm was said to have pored over volumes devoted to the occult and the arcane in a vain search for the answers which haunted his waking hours and disturbed his restless dreams. How could he have been tricked into gambling the destiny of his 60 million subjects in a war that Germany had blundered into? And why did he squander his opportunities during the stalemate on the Western Front, which gave the Americans time to enter decisively on the side of the Allies? Moreover, how did Germany lose the war after having won several significant battles?

Such matters were soon to preoccupy his successor, Adolf Hitler, whose initial aim was to avenge the 'betrayal' of 1918 and restore national pride, but whose inherent flaws made him a more suitable vessel for malevolent spirits who were drawn by the aura of resentment and repressed aggression surrounding the wounded German psyche and, once admitted, would possess it. Hitler was sufficiently shrewd not to lay the blame on imaginary secret societies. His choice of scapegoats proved to be targets who were conveniently out in the open, readily identifiable (according to Nazi racist ideology) and could be eliminated without fear of the civilian population raising a finger to protest. The Jews had been portrayed in propaganda films and even in children's schoolbooks as vermin spreading disease and corrupting the pure Aryan soul; the capitalists had been blamed by the Nazi press for the rampant inflation of the 1920s; and the communists had been demonized for organizing industrial unrest which threatened the stability of the state. The average German would be glad to see the back of all of them. The communists might put up a fight, but the SA, who were spoiling for a brawl, vastly outnumbered them. The Jews could be persuaded to accept 'resettlement', but they would have to surrender their property in exchange for the promise of safe passage. In this way, evil crept insidiously into German society, drop by drop, like a slow poison lulling the conscience of the nation into a coma.

THE NATURE OF EVIL

Whether one believes in evil as a conscious entity or defines it as a lack of empathy – the denial of the divine in oneself and others – Spence was spot on when he noted:

> '... *evil seeks its like, its own reflection in its ministers, It is indeed its prime imperfection that it is doomed to work with tools whose temper is as unsound as its own – implements which outwardly seem trenchant and effective, but which, with the impact of use soon lose their keenness and reveal the baseness of their alloy. The whole history of evil shows that it is capable of functioning only by fits*

and starts, that it does not possess the reserves and staying power of its opposite, and that, though its purpose and impulse are timeless, its vigour and judgement are unequal to the full achievement of its designs.'

Evil people are capable of wreaking havoc and causing suffering on a vast scale, but they are by definition self-centred and therefore self-defeating which ensures that they are fated to fail. Evil can only succeed in the short term and only if there is a lack of determination to limit the damage that its agents can do. The Allies sorely lacked this resolve when Hitler began to assert the German people's need for *Lebensraum* (living space) in the mid-1930s. The French in particular were weary of war and the British buzzword for the period was 'appeasement'. It was no secret that certain elements of European society and an influential section in America openly admired Hitler for the economic miracle he had apparently been able to create (by excessive borrowing with no intention of repaying the loans) and for his firm stance on the Jews. In this atmosphere of grudging respect the Nazis were able to tear up the punitive Versailles Treaty, order massive rearmament under the noses of the Allies and take back the Rhineland in 1936 without a shot being fired. Tragically, the Second World War could have been averted at this point if France had opposed the re-occupation of the Rhineland. German officers had orders to withdraw their troops if the French army deployed their forces to the region. But they remained in their barracks.

Having tested the Allies' resolve and found them wanting, Hitler went on to successfully demand the annexation of Austria, the return of the Sudetenland, the Danzig corridor and, finally, neutral Czechoslovakia before the Allies realized how foolishly naïve they had been and announced they would stand by Poland in the event of a German invasion. But by then, short of declaring a full-scale war, it was too late to stop Nazi aggression.

It is true that the evil nature of the Nazi regime was not fully revealed until the liberation of the concentration camps in 1945, but only the most ignorant and callous individual could have protested that they had no idea what a fascist dictatorship would be capable of. As the saying goes, 'It only requires good men to do nothing for evil to exist.' But is the notion of evil merely a convenient explanation for abhorrent human behaviour, a concept which serves as an excuse for not taking action or responsibility because we imagine it to be something beyond our control? Or is there evidence that evil exists as a malign and conscious influence using criminals and tyrants as its agents? With regard to the charge that the Nazi hierarchy were servants of Satan, Spence observed:

'Unless there had been a continuous tradition of evil, a steadily cumulative growth of its powers and a definite and official leadership to put them into practice, it could never have seized its opportunities so skilfully or appropriately, or have capitalized on them so successfully.'

He noted that the deities of the world's religions do not manifest themselves to their worshippers and therefore why should Lucifer do otherwise? Nazism, he explained, was not initiated by Satanists but infiltrated by them so that it could become their instrument for chaos and destruction.

> *'The process is as old as history. But history cannot remember a period nor a condition so appropriate to or so promising for the achievement of the grand Satanic purpose as those which presented themselves in Germany between the years 1920 and 1940.'*

In Spence's eyes, Nazi Germany was the very personification of Faust, selling its soul for temporal power.

> *'That pride which is the basis of the Satanic heresy, is pre-eminently developed in the Nazi creed, along with its concordant vices of mendacity, subtle and cowardly distortion of the truth, assassination open and secret, the massacre and persecution of the helpless – in a word, unbridled diabolic licence ... If the Prince of Darkness in person had undertaken to govern that nation it is difficult to suggest how he could have borne himself otherwise than its unhappy leader has done, or with more fantastic wickedness.'*

FIGHTING THE GOOD FIGHT

Spence and his occult colleagues were not the only people to express the belief that Germany had sold its soul to the dark side. The most vociferous critics of the Nazi regime repeatedly spoke in apocalyptic terms. The exiled Queen Wilhelmina of the Netherlands described the war as being 'between God and conscience and the forces of darkness', while Cardinal Hinsley, Archbishop of Westminster, told his congregation, 'You are on the side of the angels in the struggle against the pride of rebellious Lucifer.' The Anglican Bishop of Ipswich, Dr W. G. Whittingham, was equally convinced of the righteousness of the Allied cause and the nature of the threat posed by their enemies. 'We are not fighting flesh and blood,' he wrote, 'but the devil, in the persons of Hitler and his gang.'

Such warnings were not merely biblical rhetoric. Many of those living under Nazi occupation or who sheltered from the falling bombs of the Luftwaffe were sincere in their belief that they were resisting evil incarnate. It was only later, when they learned of the scale of Nazi atrocities from the cinema newsreels and from the lips of the victims during their testimony at Nuremberg, that they realized the terrible truth – that human beings are capable of truly evil acts even without the urging of external influences. So many of the concentration camp commandants and the bureaucrats who ordered the transportations to Auschwitz, Treblinka and Dachau lacked the imagination to realize the awful consequences of their actions. Others simply didn't care. They were devoid of conscience and compassion. A few even believed that they were acting for the greater good. This wilful indifference to the suffering of others gave rise to what became known as 'the banality of evil' and it explains the otherwise incomprehensible actions of serial killers and habitual criminals today as it did the actions of those complicit in the genocide effected by the Third Reich.

The lone voice of the anti-Nazi student organization, the White Rose, failed to prick the conscience of those who acquiesced in the crimes perpetrated by Hitler's thugs. Its young leaders were beheaded for merely having the temerity to voice opposition to the regime. But they willingly sacrificed themselves in a vain effort to awaken their countrymen to the nature of the contagion that had corrupted them, which encouraged children to inform on their parents and the spiteful to denounce their neighbours. One of their pamphlets expressed openly what many must have feared even to think.

'Every word that comes from Hitler's mouth is a lie. When he says peace, he means war, and when he blasphemously uses the name of the Almighty, he means the power of evil, the fallen angel, Satan. His mouth is the foul-smelling maw of Hell, and his might is at bottom accursed. True, we must conduct a struggle against the National Socialist terrorist state with rational means; but whoever today still doubts the reality, the existence of demonic powers, has failed by a wide margin to understand the metaphysical background of this war. Behind the concrete, the visible

events, behind all objective, logical considerations, we find the irrational element: the struggle against the demon, against the servants of the Antichrist. Everywhere and at all times demons have been lurking in the dark, waiting for the moment when man is weak; when of his own volition he leaves his place in the order of Creation as founded for him by God in freedom; when he yields to the force of evil, separates himself from the powers of a higher order; and after voluntarily taking the first step, he is driven on to the next and the next at a furiously accelerating rate.'

Few voices were raised against the Nazis. In fact, the Nazification of Germany was enforced at every level of society. Youngsters were even taught to use 'the German greeting' in primary school.

The German people's apparent acceptance of the demonic as a conscious, influential entity was not solely the result of centuries of indoctrination by the Church. German intellectuals, writers and artists of both the Romantic era and the Rational reactionary period had acknowledged the existence of evil as a latent force within each and every individual. Goethe (in *Dichtung und Wahrheit [Poetry and Truth]*) gave one of the most penetrating insights into the true nature of evil as it was to manifest in Adolf Hitler when he wrote:

> *'This daemonic element manifests itself in all corporeal and incorporeal things, and even expresses itself most distinctly in animals, yet it is primarily in its relation to man that we observe its mysterious workings ... But the most fearful manifestation of the daemonic is when it is predominating in some individual character ... Such persons are not always the most eminent men, either in intellect or special gifts, and they are seldom distinguished by goodness of heart; a tremendous energy seems to emanate from them, and they exercise a wonderful power over all creatures and even over the elements; and indeed, who shall say how much further such influence may extend? All the moral powers combined are no avail against them; in vain does the more enlightened portion of mankind attempt to throw suspicion upon them as dupes or as deceivers – the masses are attracted by them. Seldom or ever do they find their equals among their contemporaries; nothing can vanquish*

them but the Universe itself, with which they have begun
the fray; and it is from observation of facts such as these
that the strange but tremendous saying has arisen, "Nemo
contra Deum nisi Deus ipse" [Nobody can be against the
Divine Will but God himself].'

In other words, evil is merely the contrary impulse to evolution
which manifests in man as the traditional vices. In modern
psychological terms it is the result of an unbalanced psyche
due to an inflated ego which distorts the person's perception of
the world, like a spoilt child who believes he is the centre of
the universe. But during times of national crisis, such as in the
early years of the Second World War, the combatants found it
necessary to create an archetypal image of their enemy as evil
incarnate in order to justify the act of killing which in peacetime
would have been a crime and a cardinal sin.

But there were many who dismissed such rational
explanations and persisted in their belief in the existence of
demons and devils because they were far easier to accept than
intellectual concepts such as the ego, the superego and the id.
Occultist Lewis Spence wrote:

'*As Adolf Hitler has advanced in life there has steadily*
grown up within him another man, rather an evil spirit, of
the most violent and deadly kind, to whose daily expansion
he has offered little or no resistance. In a word, the malign
power has seen in this base and pitiless creature, utterly

lost to all human sensibility, and moved only by crude and elementary emotions of revenge and mock sentiment, precisely the kind of vehicle which it sought, and which it ever seeks to carry out its infernal purpose … That he is impelled by forces the true nature of which he does not comprehend is plainly obvious from the account of those conversations he held with Sir Neville Henderson before the outbreak of war, which makes it evident that he is under the domination of influences of which he is only the mouthpiece.'

Spence assumed that the lengthy silences with which Hitler was known to precede every significant decision betrayed the fact that he was listening for the inner voice.

'His mind and will are, in a word, at the mercy of that force which, throughout the ages, has masqueraded under many names, but which, nevertheless, has only one identity … his Luciferian master who is eternally incapable of speaking the truth …'

Such beliefs persist to this day.

A CATHEDRAL OF LIGHT

The following account of the climax to the 1936 Nuremberg Rally is taken from the official party account of the event,

Offizieller Bericht über den Verlauf des Reichsparteitages mit sämtlichen Kongressreden (Munich: Zentralverlag der NSDAP) [Translated by C. Roland].

'The Nuremberg Party Rally concluded on Friday evening with an impressive roll call of political leaders. As the setting sun cast its red radiance over the towers of Nuremberg, 90,000 of Adolf Hitler's followers and 25,000 flag-bearers marched in wide columns to the Dutzendteich. All Nuremberg was alert to witness the impressive spectacle.

'Shortly before 7.30 when it is almost dark, a floodlight shines into the sky. The spotlights illuminate more than 200 swastika banners that flutter from 12-metre high flagpoles in the evening breeze. Suddenly one senses the enormous scale of the field and absorbs the memorable image. More lights illuminate the white marble podium, a fantastic, unforgettable sight. All those present stand in hushed silence and motionless in awe of the beauty of the scene. The greatest of the Führer's stately buildings on the Nuremberg Reich Party Rally grounds is revealed in all its glory.

'More lights sweep the field, revealing the limitless brown columns, demonstrating their precision marching, until suddenly, at a command, all 90,000 are in position. A celebratory mood electrifies everyone, as they anticipate the experience that awaits them. But they cannot imagine what will actually happen.

Pomp and pageantry Nazi-style: the 'Old Fighters' of the SA parade at Nuremberg.

'Orders come from the loudspeakers, vehicles race everywhere. Moments before 8 o'clock, the spotlights at the southern end of the stadium dim. This is where the Führer will make his entrance.

'The familiar cries that accompany the Führer's arrival echo from the Dutzendteich train station. The procession circles the field, then suddenly 180,000 people look to the stars. A hundred and fifty blue spotlights send their beams hundreds of metres into the sky to form the most impressive cathedral that mortals will ever see. There, at the entrance, we have the first sight of the Führer. He stands motionless looking upwards, then turns and strides past the long columns of his loyal fighters, 20 deep, with his aides following behind. A sea of cries of "Heil" and euphoria erupts around him. Stars sparkle through the deep blue curtain of the cathedral of light, and the emblems of the German nation billow in the soft breeze.'

THE NUREMBERG RITUALS – AN INVOCATION OF MARS

'They conjure up the demonic powers of the ancient Germanic pantheon and because that lust for fight comes alive in them which we find in the ancient Germans … a spectacle will be performed in Germany, compared with which the French Revolution may look like an innocent idyll.'

Heinrich Heine (1835)

To the uninitiated, the Nuremberg rallies represented a celebration of German nationalism, an adoration of the Führer and an impressive display of military might. But they were much more than elaborately staged spectacles. They were a 'triumph of the will', to borrow the title of Leni Riefenstahl's film documenting the 1934 Nazi party rally, and an invocation of Mars, the pagan God of War.

Hitler may have been an ill-educated Bohemian driven by the basest human instincts, but he intuitively knew how to exploit his innate capacity for manipulating the masses into acting as a mindless mob. He was also shrewd enough to understand that the power of his personality was not enough to induce even his most fervent followers to swear undying allegiance to their flag, their Führer or the Fatherland. He needed to involve them in a formalized ritual so that their fate would be allied to his – for better or for worse.

This was the true purpose of the Nuremberg rallies. They acted as an insidious form of quasi-religious magic ritual, a perversion of both the Catholic sacrament and a pagan consecration of the weapons with which Nazi Germany would wage war, with Hitler as High Priest and his inner circle in the role of acolytes. It was not necessary for the participants to be aware of the part they were playing. They were simply swept along on a tide of heightened emotion expertly and cynically stage-managed by Hitler's architect, Albert Speer, who understood the seductive power of making each member of the crowd believe that they were participating in a heroic Wagnerian pageant, and so had

Rapt attention: massed ranks of soldiers listen to a speech at the 1934 Nuremberg Rally.

become part of something greater than themselves. All of the elements for invoking the dark side of the psyche were harnessed by Speer to focus the mass ranks of the Führer's followers on a single purpose – the awakening of the collective will.

The stadium formed a magic circle from which non-believers were excluded. Within this sacred space the crowds were whipped up into an ecstasy of expectation by ritual drumming, blaring fanfares, fluttering banners and the sight of massed ranks of black-shirted SS troops and brown-shirted SA stormtroopers marching with automated precision. This was designed to impress upon the onlookers the idea that they were privileged to be allowed to participate, that they were elite initiates of a special order and invincible so long as they remained loyal.

The basic human need to conform was ruthlessly exploited with each section afforded their own uniforms, awards, ritual ceremonies and insignia. Even the women and children were made to join the Hitler Youth and the BDM (*Bund Deutscher Mädchen* – the League of German Girls).

As the crowds waited in the hot sun, Wagner's music evoked 'racial memories' of Nordic heroes and the mythic tradition of Aryan supremacy after which stirring marches boasted of military glory yet to come. Banners of red, white and black fluttered in the afternoon breeze – the traditional colours of war, terror and death.

The late arrival of the Führer was designed for maximum impact, his arrival triggering a release of tension and idol worship akin to a modern rock concert.

Albert Speer's 'Cathedral of Light', the crowning moment of the Nuremberg Rally, 1937. Speer was Hitler's favourite architect, and would go on to become his Minister of Armaments.

Overlooking the ceremony stood the high priests of this black order, Hitler's inner circle. This hierarchy was designed to give the illusion of order and of unity. In truth, Hitler's acolytes were a self-serving rabble who would have turned on each other had it not been for the overbearing personality of the Führer holding his squabbling brood together.

As dusk descended on the stadium, 200 searchlights were aimed at the sky to form what Speer called 'a Cathedral of Light'. His words were well chosen. Clearly the purpose had been to create the illusion of a magical temple. It only lacked the climactic act, a blood sacrifice, to seal the pact with the dark forces they had invoked. In its place Hitler consecrated the flags of new SS battalions by bringing them together with the sacred 'blood banner' that had been carried in the failed Munich Putsch of 1923 and which was stained with the blood of Nazi martyrs as the crowd responded with hoarse cries of *Sieg Heil*. There would be time enough for blood sacrifice in the years to come on a scale undreamt of by even their most bloodthirsty forebears.

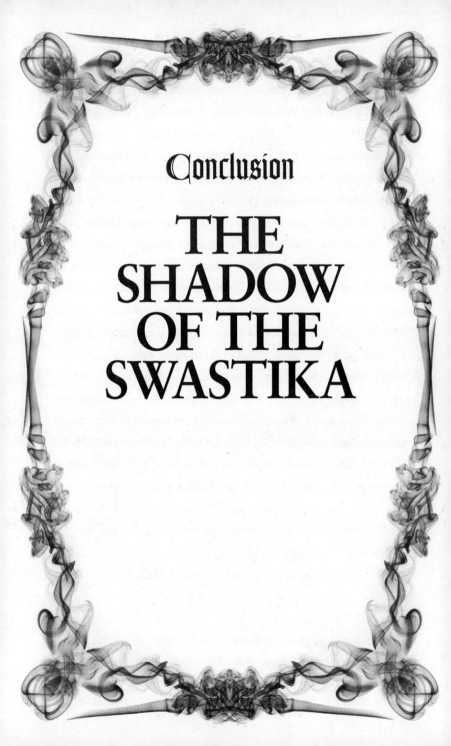

Conclusion

THE
SHADOW
OF THE
SWASTIKA

ontrary to popular myth there is no documentary evidence to support the belief that Hitler and his inner circle were practising magicians or occultists of any kind. In fact, Hitler is on record as having expressed his contempt for the *völkisch* occultists of the *Germanenorden* and their Wotan-worshipping brethren. If the Nazis had been the devil's disciples, why did they not proclaim their allegiance in 1940 when they had conquered most of Europe as proof that their dark lord and master was superior to the Judaeo-Christian God? Instead, they talked of supplanting the Church with their own neo-pagan religion which, as any nature-loving pagan knows, is not the same as Satanism – quite the contrary in fact. Those who persist in their belief that Hitler was a practitioner of the black arts and that Himmler was his high priest argue that all magicians – and Satanists in particular – are expressly forbidden to speak of their practices to anyone other than fellow initiates. And in support of this, they cite the magician's credo: 'To dare, to will, to know and to remain silent.' However, neither the notorious Aleister Crowley nor self-confessed Satanist Anton LaVey, the two most vociferous exponents of the dark arts in modern times, felt it necessary to adhere to that dictum.

Neither is there any anecdotal evidence to support the claims made by crypto-historians who have attempted to re-write history with the Nazis recast as willing instruments of unnameable 'dark forces'. While it is a matter of record that the Nazis financed expeditions to Tibet and other supposed centres of esoteric power in search of holy artefacts, they did so primarily to establish a connection between Germans and 'Aryans', a racial rather than a religious quest. Such distorted images have taken root because for decades mainstream historians relied on two primary sources to prove the extent of the Nazis' obsession with the occult, both of which are highly dubious to say the least.

Hermann Rauschning's fabricated memoirs have provided a wealth of fictitious quotes in which Hitler revealed a familiarity with esoteric lore, but recently it came to light that the former *Gauleiter* had only met his Führer on one occasion and that was only briefly. At no time did Rauschning have a private audience with Hitler as he had claimed.

Equally misleading has been Trevor Ravenscroft's unquestionably fictional account of Hitler's occult initiation, *The Spear of Destiny*, which was published and accepted as fact, allegedly against the author's wishes. But, as this present work has demonstrated, Hitler had neither the self-discipline nor the inclination to follow the so-called Left-Hand Path. Even if he had aspirations to ally himself with diabolical forces he would have proven a poor pupil. It is a fallacy that black magicians simply submit to the dark side or sell their souls in a Faustian pact with the devil and are instantly granted access to forbidden knowledge and power. Every magician, black or white, must first master the mental disciplines of meditation and creative visualization to open their Third Eye, the organ of psychic sensitivity and thereafter practise such demanding tasks as the creation of thought forms. It is only after many years of rigorous training and devotion to the Work, or the Mysteries, as they are called in esoteric circles, that the initiate can choose which path to follow – the path of self-realization and selfless service or the path of self-serving self-indulgence. Of course, those who elect to take the Left-Hand Path do not consider themselves evil in the traditional sense of the word. They believe that they have the right to do as they will, as the notorious Aleister Crowley termed it, and that by doing so they are merely asserting their contempt for the constraints and superstitious conventions of orthodox religion.

And this is the point at which the paths of the satanic magician and Adolf Hitler and his associates converge. For while it is indisputable that Hitler and the Nazis were not active disciples of the devil, they did indulge their basest instincts and satiated their sadistic appetites to the detriment of their true nature or Higher Self. In this sense what these men did and became was the very definition of evil. They suppressed their own humanity and refused to see it in their victims. Moreover, they corrupted others, some by force, others by simply sanctioning their acts of brutality on their former neighbours and fellow countrymen who were deemed unworthy of the right to life. Some of the worst excesses of the Nazi era were carried out by ordinary men and women who were encouraged to give vent to their spite and vindictiveness free of the threat of reprisal or the prospect of being brought to account for their actions. This was possible because both the perpetrators of these crimes and their Nazi masters considered themselves to be beyond Good and Evil.

In short, the Nazi regime was capable of unleashing the torments of hell without assistance from supernatural forces. But that does not mean that such forces were not at work in the world at that time, only that they were not in a form which we would understand or recognize as demonic.

The aim of ceremonial magic is the focusing of an adept's will to bring about a change in consciousness or to effect a change in their environment. The Nazis were practitioners of magic in its truest and purest sense, but they did so unconsciously. And because they were unaware of what they were doing and the nature of the forces they had unleashed, they found they were unable to control it and consequently were consumed by it. It is not by chance that documentary filmmaker Leni Refenstal's record of the 1934 Nuremberg Rally was entitled *Triumph of the Will*, for the focusing of willpower is the core element and key to successful magic.

Hitler was not a magician, nor was he the messiah the German mystics had prophesied. He was a true *Untermensch*, to use the Nazi term, the type of low, undeveloped personality which allows itself to be driven by its instincts rather than intuition, the embodiment of the elemental force psychoanalysts call the ego and which occultists term the Lower Self. In Jewish mysticism, Satan simply means 'tempter' and is symbolic of our shadow self, the dark side of the psyche, while the concept of the demon came from a corruption of *daimon*, the Greek word for the human soul. The devils and demons of medieval magic are the creation of the early Church – they do not appear in the

Old Testament. There were conceived to put the fear of God into potential sinners and give the Church the means to enrich itself by selling absolution from the fires of purgatory. Later they served to keep society on the straight and narrow until a body of civil laws could be formulated. Today they serve no purpose other than as symbols of our fears and addictions. No one of sane mind has claimed to have seen a demon or the devil since the Dark Ages. Hitler never spoke of having heard demonic voices urging him to offer a blood sacrifice to his infernal master.

The Nazis consciously chose to awaken the demonic side of their people's psyche for their own selfish ends. It was not fate or destiny which put Germany on the path to self-destruction, but the wilfulness of their leadership and the willingness of the people to submit to that greater will. Other nations suffered from high unemployment and escalating inflation during the 1930s and no doubt a proportion of their citizens were anti-Semites, but only Germany set out to make itself master of the world and rid itself of 'the Jewish problem'. For twelve terrible years they ruled through fear, distrust, deception and brutality. The Nazi state was George Orwell's nightmare scenario made manifest, 'a boot stamping on a human face forever'.

Esoteric doctrine states that every individual has the opportunity to make their own heaven and hell on Earth during their allotted lifetime. Hitler chose the latter and in doing so proved to the world that evil is entirely man-made and those who succumb to it are doomed to failure. Unfortunately, there are still those in the world today who have not learned the lessons of history. Until they do, the shadow of the swastika will continue to darken this world.

'This institution supports the Führer unconditionally.'
The banner on Wittenau Lunatic Asylum, 1938

Timeline

1889–1933

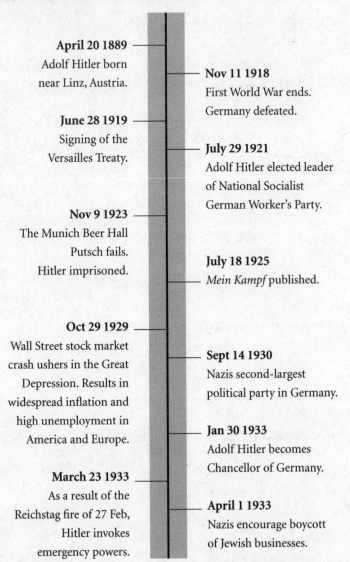

April 20 1889
Adolf Hitler born
near Linz, Austria.

Nov 11 1918
First World War ends.
Germany defeated.

June 28 1919
Signing of the
Versailles Treaty.

July 29 1921
Adolf Hitler elected leader
of National Socialist
German Worker's Party.

Nov 9 1923
The Munich Beer Hall
Putsch fails.
Hitler imprisoned.

July 18 1925
Mein Kampf published.

Oct 29 1929
Wall Street stock market
crash ushers in the Great
Depression. Results in
widespread inflation and
high unemployment in
America and Europe.

Sept 14 1930
Nazis second-largest
political party in Germany.

Jan 30 1933
Adolf Hitler becomes
Chancellor of Germany.

March 23 1933
As a result of the
Reichstag fire of 27 Feb,
Hitler invokes
emergency powers.

April 1 1933
Nazis encourage boycott
of Jewish businesses.

TIMELINE

TIMELINE
1933–1938

May 10 1933
Ritual book burning in
German cities.

July 14 1933
Nazis outlaw opposition
parties.

June 30 1934
'The Night of the Long
Knives'

July 25 1934
Nazis murder Austrian
Chancellor Dollfuss.

Aug 2 1934
Death of German President
von Hindenburg

Aug 19 1934
Adolf Hitler is confirmed as
Führer.

Sept 15 1935
Nuremberg Race Laws deny
Jews equal rights.

March 7 1936
German troops occupy the
Rhineland unopposed.

July 18 1936
Civil war in Spain. Fascists
under Franco receive
military aid from Germany.

Aug 1 1936
Olympic games open in
Berlin.

June 11 1937
Soviet army severely
weakened and demoralized
after Stalin instigates purge
of senior Red Army officers.

March 12 1938
Germany's *Anschluss*
(union) with Austria.

TIMELINE
1938–1939

Sept 30 1938

British Prime Minister Neville Chamberlain signs Munich Agreement guaranteeing Britain and her Allies will not intervene if Hitler 'reclaims' the Sudetenland. Chamberlain claims he has secured 'peace in our time' by appeasing Hitler and preventing a European war.

Oct 15 1938
German troops occupy the Sudetenland.

Nov 9 1938
Kristallnacht (The Night of Broken Glass). Throughout Germany, Nazi thugs and their supporters smash the windows of Jewish businesses and set synagogues on fire.

March 15–16 1939
Nazis take Czechoslovakia.

March 28 1939
Spanish Civil War ends Franco's fascists take power.

May 22 1939
Nazis sign 'Pact of Steel'with Italy.

Aug 23 1939
Nazis and Soviets sign Nonaggression Pact, leaving Germany free to attack the West without fear of a second front being opened up to the east.

Aug 25 1939
In response Britain and Poland sign a Mutual Assistance Treaty.

Sept 1 1939
Nazis invade Poland.

TIMELINE
1939–1940

Sept 3 1939
Britain, France, Australia and New Zealand declare war on Germany.

Sept 17 1939
Soviet Army invades Poland. Ten days later, Poland surrenders.

Sept 29 1939
Nazis and Soviets divide up Poland.

October 1939
Nazis instigate policy of euthanasia. The sick and disabled are exterminated.

Nov 8 1939
Assassination attempt on Hitler fails.

Nov 30 1939
Soviet Army invades Finland. On 12 March, Finland signs a peace treaty.

April 9 1940
Nazis invade Denmark and Norway.

May 10 1940
Blitzkrieg! Nazis invade France, Belgium, Luxembourg and the Netherlands. Winston Churchill appointed British Prime Minister.

May 15 1940
The Netherlands surrenders. Belgium capitulates on May 28.

May 26 1940
Evacuation of Allied troops from Dunkirk. Ends June 3.

TIMELINE
1940–1940

June 10 1940
Norway surrenders; Italy declares war on Britain and France.

June 14 1940
German troops enter Paris

June 16 1940
Marshal Pétain becomes French Prime Minister.

June 18 1940
Hitler and Mussolini form alliance; Soviets occupy the Baltic States.

June 22 1940
Hitler humiliates France by forcing its leaders to sign an armistice in the same railway carriage in which Germany signed the surrender in 1918.

June 28 1940
Britain recognizes the exiled General Charles de Gaulle as the leader of the Free French. In France the 'puppet' Vichy government collaborates with the Nazis.

July 1 1940
German U-boat campaign begins in the Atlantic harassing merchant convoys bringing vital supplies to the British Isles.

July 10 1940
Battle of Britain begins. Throughout August, German bombers target British airfields and factories. The British respond by bombing Berlin – the first long-range raid of the war.

Sept 13 1940
Italians invade Egypt.

TIMELINE
1940–1941

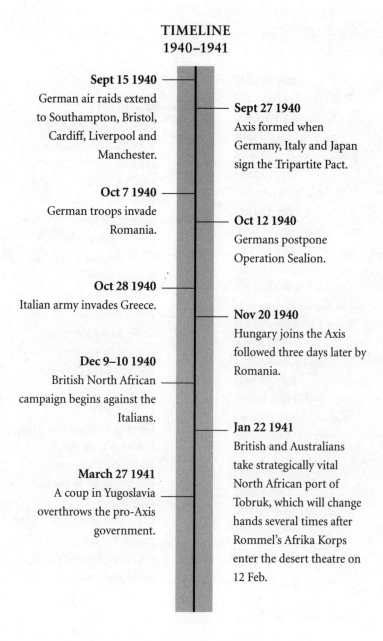

Sept 15 1940
German air raids extend
to Southampton, Bristol,
Cardiff, Liverpool and
Manchester.

Sept 27 1940
Axis formed when
Germany, Italy and Japan
sign the Tripartite Pact.

Oct 7 1940
German troops invade
Romania.

Oct 12 1940
Germans postpone
Operation Sealion.

Oct 28 1940
Italian army invades Greece.

Nov 20 1940
Hungary joins the Axis
followed three days later by
Romania.

Dec 9–10 1940
British North African
campaign begins against the
Italians.

Jan 22 1941
British and Australians
take strategically vital
North African port of
Tobruk, which will change
hands several times after
Rommel's Afrika Korps
enter the desert theatre on
12 Feb.

March 27 1941
A coup in Yugoslavia
overthrows the pro-Axis
government.

TIMELINE
1941–1941

April 6 1941

Nazis invade Greece and Yugoslavia. The latter surrenders on 17 April. Greece surrenders ten days later.

May 10 1941

Deputy Führer Rudolf Hess flies to Scotland and is arrested.

May 27 1941

Nazi flagship, the *Bismarck*, sunk by the British Navy.

June 1941

Nazi SS *Einsatzgruppen* begin programme of mass murder in Latvia.

June 22 1941

German invasion of Soviet Union codenamed Operation Barbarossa.

July 3 1941

Stalin orders a 'scorched earth' policy in the face of the advancing Germans.

July 12 1941

British and Soviets sign Mutual Assistance Agreement.

July 31 1941

Goering instructs Heydrich to instigate the 'Final Solution' – the mass extermination of the Jews in Germany.

Sept 1 1941

Nazis order Jews to wear yellow stars.

Sept 3 1941

First experimental use of gas chambers at Auschwitz.

TIMELINE
1941–1942

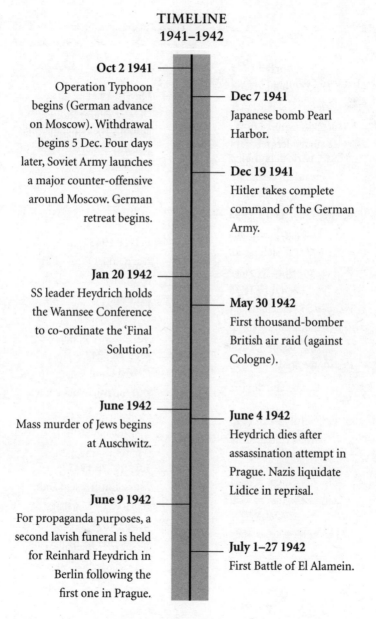

Oct 2 1941
Operation Typhoon begins (German advance on Moscow). Withdrawal begins 5 Dec. Four days later, Soviet Army launches a major counter-offensive around Moscow. German retreat begins.

Dec 7 1941
Japanese bomb Pearl Harbor.

Dec 19 1941
Hitler takes complete command of the German Army.

Jan 20 1942
SS leader Heydrich holds the Wannsee Conference to co-ordinate the 'Final Solution'.

May 30 1942
First thousand-bomber British air raid (against Cologne).

June 1942
Mass murder of Jews begins at Auschwitz.

June 4 1942
Heydrich dies after assassination attempt in Prague. Nazis liquidate Lidice in reprisal.

June 9 1942
For propaganda purposes, a second lavish funeral is held for Reinhard Heydrich in Berlin following the first one in Prague.

July 1–27 1942
First Battle of El Alamein.

TIMELINE
1942–1943

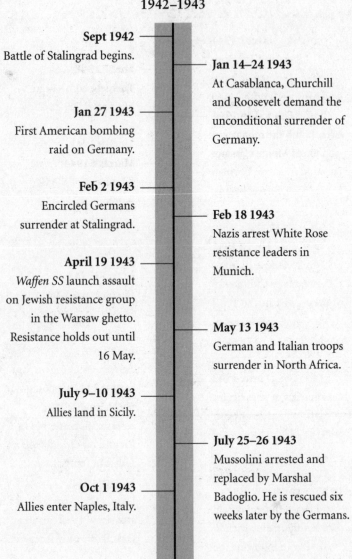

Sept 1942
Battle of Stalingrad begins.

Jan 14–24 1943
At Casablanca, Churchill
and Roosevelt demand the
unconditional surrender of
Germany.

Jan 27 1943
First American bombing
raid on Germany.

Feb 2 1943
Encircled Germans
surrender at Stalingrad.

Feb 18 1943
Nazis arrest White Rose
resistance leaders in
Munich.

April 19 1943
Waffen SS launch assault
on Jewish resistance group
in the Warsaw ghetto.
Resistance holds out until
16 May.

May 13 1943
German and Italian troops
surrender in North Africa.

July 9–10 1943
Allies land in Sicily.

July 25–26 1943
Mussolini arrested and
replaced by Marshal
Badoglio. He is rescued six
weeks later by the Germans.

Oct 1 1943
Allies enter Naples, Italy.

TIMELINE
1943–1944

Jan 22 1944
Allies land at Anzio.

Jan 27 1944
The siege of Leningrad is
lifted after 900 days.

Feb 15–18 1944
Allies bomb the monastery
of Monte Cassino.

March 4 1944
First major daylight
bombing raid on Berlin by
the Allies.

June 5 1944
Allies enter Rome.

June 6 1944
D-Day landings.

June 13 1944
First German V1 rocket
attack on Britain.

June 22 1944
The Soviet summer
offensive begins the rout of
the German invaders.

July 3 1944
'Battle of the Hedgerows'
in Normandy. A week later,
Caen is liberated.

July 20 1944
Hitler survives assassination
attempt at the 'Wolf's Lair'
HQ.

TIMELINE
1944–1945

July 24 1944
Soviet troops liberate first
concentration camp at
Majdanek.

Aug 25 1944
Paris liberated.

Sept 13 1944
US troops reach the
Siegfried Line.

Sept 17 1944
Operation Market Garden
begins (Allied airborne
assault on the Netherlands).

Oct 2 1944
Polish Army forced to
surrender to the Germans
in Warsaw after weeks of
heroic resistance.

Oct 14 1944
Allies liberate Athens;
Rommel commits suicide
on Hitler's orders for his
part in the July plot.

Dec 16–27 1944
Battle of the Bulge in
the Ardennes. Retreating
Waffen SS murder 84 US
POWs at Malmedy.

Dec 26 1944
The 'Battling Bastards
of Bastogne' relieved
by General Patton. The
Germans withdraw from
the Ardennes during
January. Hitler's last gamble
has failed.

Jan 27 1945
Soviet troops liberate
Auschwitz.

TIMELINE
1945–1945

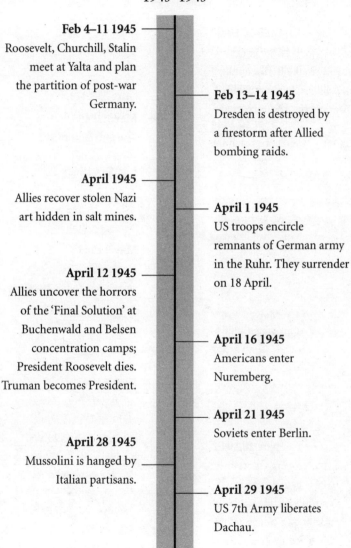

Feb 4–11 1945
Roosevelt, Churchill, Stalin
meet at Yalta and plan
the partition of post-war
Germany.

Feb 13–14 1945
Dresden is destroyed by
a firestorm after Allied
bombing raids.

April 1945
Allies recover stolen Nazi
art hidden in salt mines.

April 1 1945
US troops encircle
remnants of German army
in the Ruhr. They surrender
on 18 April.

April 12 1945
Allies uncover the horrors
of the 'Final Solution' at
Buchenwald and Belsen
concentration camps;
President Roosevelt dies.
Truman becomes President.

April 16 1945
Americans enter
Nuremberg.

April 21 1945
Soviets enter Berlin.

April 28 1945
Mussolini is hanged by
Italian partisans.

April 29 1945
US 7th Army liberates
Dachau.

TIMELINE
1945–1945

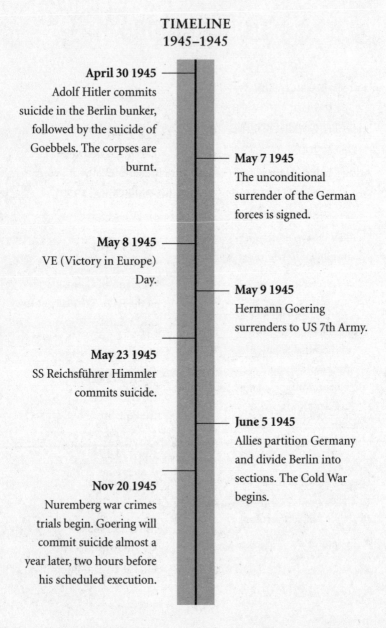

April 30 1945
Adolf Hitler commits suicide in the Berlin bunker, followed by the suicide of Goebbels. The corpses are burnt.

May 7 1945
The unconditional surrender of the German forces is signed.

May 8 1945
VE (Victory in Europe) Day.

May 9 1945
Hermann Goering surrenders to US 7th Army.

May 23 1945
SS Reichsführer Himmler commits suicide.

June 5 1945
Allies partition Germany and divide Berlin into sections. The Cold War begins.

Nov 20 1945
Nuremberg war crimes trials begin. Goering will commit suicide almost a year later, two hours before his scheduled execution.

Bibliography

E. Amy Buller, *Darkness Over Germany* (Longmans, Green and Co, 1943)

Nicholas Goodric-Clarke, *The Occult Roots of Nazism* (Tauris Parke, 2005)

Adolf Hitler, *Mein Kampf* (Random House, 1992)

Stuart Holroyd, *Psychic Voyage* (Aldus Publishing, 1977)

Aldous Huxley, *The Doors of Perception* (Vintage, 2004)

Dr Felix Jay, article in *Traditional Astrologer* magazine (1998)

Francis King, *Satan and Swastika* (Granada Publications, 1976)

Peter Levenda, *Unholy Alliance* (Continuum, 2002)

Friedrich Nietzsche, *The AntiChrist* (Prometheus, 2000)

Friedrich Nietzsche, *Beyond Good and Evil* (Dover, 1989)

Friedrich Nietzsche, *Thus Spake Zarathustra* (Penguin, 1989)

John Pearson, *The Life of Ian Fleming* (Companion Book Club, 1966)

Nigel Pennick, *Hitler's Secret Sciences* (Neville Spearman, 1981)

Hermann Rauschning, *Hitler Speaks* (Howard Fertig, 1939)

Hermann Rauschning, *Voice of Destruction* (Kessinger, 2004)

Trevor Ravenscroft, *The Spear of Destiny* (Sphere, 1990)

Walter Schellenberg, *Memoirs* (Andre Deutsch, 2006)

William L. Shirer, *The Rise and Fall of the Third Reich* (Arrow, 1991)

Albert Speer, *Inside The Third Reich* (Weidenfeld and Nicholson, 2003)

Lewis Spence, 'Occult Causes of the Present War' (Kessinger, 1998)

Gerald Suster, *Hitler and the Age of Horus* (Sphere, 1981)

John Symonds, *The Medusa's Head* (Mandrake Press, 1991)

Robert G.L. Waite, *The Psychopathic God* (Basic Books, 1977)

Wilhelm Wulff, *Zodiac and Swastika* (Barker, 1973)

Index

Picture Credits